U0802261

2009

中国国际收支报告

China's Balance of Payments Report

国家外汇管理局国际收支分析小组
BOP Analysis Group of
State Administration of Foreign Exchange

中国金融出版社
China Financial Publishing House

责任编辑：张翠华
责任校对：刘　明
责任印制：裴　刚

图书在版编目（CIP）数据

2009 中国国际收支报告（2009 Zhongguo Guoji Shouzhi Baogao）/ 国家外汇管理局国际收支分析小组编．—北京：中国金融出版社，2010.8
ISBN 978-7-5049-5596-8

Ⅰ．①2… Ⅱ．①国… Ⅲ．①国际收支—研究报告—中国—2009 Ⅳ．①F812.4

中国版本图书馆 CIP 数据核字（2010）第 142147 号

出版
发行　中国金融出版社
社址　北京市丰台区益泽路 2 号
市场开发部　(010) 63272190，66070804（传真）
网上书店　http://www.chinafph.com　(010) 63286832，63365686（传真）
读者服务部　(010) 66070833，62568380
邮编　100071
经销　新华书店
印刷　北京华正印刷有限公司
尺寸　210 毫米 ×285 毫米
印张　10
字数　188 千
版次　2010 年 8 月第 1 版
印次　2010 年 8 月第 1 次印刷
印数　1—2000
定价　80.00 元
ISBN 978-7-5049-5596-8/F.5156

国家外汇管理局
国际收支分析小组人员名单

组　　长：易　纲

副 组 长：邓先宏　方上浦　王小奕　李　超　黄国波　韩玉婷

审　　稿：王允贵　张生会　王春英　谢和民　孙鲁军　崔汉忠

统　　稿：管　涛　马少波　周　济

执　　笔：

第一部分：朱至瑜　马　昀　黄　蕾　赵玉超

第二部分：姬　智　马玉娟　常国栋　胡　红　查晓阳

第三部分：温建东

第四部分：朱至瑜　马　昀

专　　栏：马　昀　马玉娟　申　觅　谢月兰　朱至瑜

附录整理：赵玉超　黄　蕾

其他提供材料的还有：朱　奇

英文翻译：周海文　谢月兰　王　亮

英文审校：Nancy Hearst（美国哈佛大学费正清东亚研究中心）

Contributors to This Report

Head
Yi Gang

Deputy Head
Deng Xianhong　Fang Shangpu　Wang Xiaoyi　Li Chao
Huang Guobo　Han Yuting

Readers
Wang Yungui　Zhang Shenghui　Wang Chunying　Xie Hemin
Sun Lujun　Cui Hanzhong

Editors
Guan Tao　Ma Shaobo　Zhou Ji

Authors
Part One: Zhu Zhiyu　Ma Yun　Huang Lei　Zhao Yuchao
Part Two: Ji Zhi　Ma Yujuan　Chang Guodong　Hu Hong
Zha Xiaoyang
Part Three: Wen Jiandong
Part Four: Zhu Zhiyu　Ma Yun
Boxes: Ma Yun　Ma Yujuan　Shen Mi　Xie Yuelan　Zhu Zhiyu

Appendix: Zhao Yuchao　Huang Lei

Other Contributors: Zhu Qi

Translators: Zhou Haiwen　Xie Yuelan　Wang Liang

Proofreader: Nancy Hearst (Fairbank Center for East Asian Research, Harvard University)

内容摘要

2009年，在世界各国大规模经济刺激政策的推动下，全球经济触底反弹，复苏迹象日益凸显。我国经济顺利度过了21世纪以来最为困难的一年，企稳向好势头更加明显。

2009年，国际金融危机影响仍然存在，我国国际收支交易活动总体上放缓，货物贸易、服务贸易、直接投资等主要项目收支规模较2008年有所下降。经常项目、资本和金融项目保持“双顺差”格局，国际收支状况继续改善，经常项目顺差与同期GDP之比为6.1%，较2008年下降3.5个百分点，连续第二年呈回落态势，净出口对我国经济增长的拉动作用为负，内需的贡献力度加大。随着国内外经济的企稳回升，外汇资金净流入规模逐步恢复，下半年国际收支总顺差高于上半年，并呈现正增长。从总体上看，当前我国国际收支顺差式失衡问题依然突出。

2010年，世界经济形势预计继续向好，发达国家经济逐步回稳，新兴市场国家将成为全球经济增长的主要动力，我国经济保持平稳较快增长，国际收支运行的宏观环境总体上将好于2009年。同时，在汇率、利率等市场因素驱动下，跨境资金流动日趋活跃，外汇资金流入我国的规模可能增加。但随着调结构、促转变政策的逐步到位，经常项目顺差与GDP的比例可能进一步下降，国内机构对外投资保持一定规模，我国国际收支状况有望继续改善。

下一阶段，我国更加注重经济发展方式的转变和经济结构的调整，外汇管理工作将全面贯彻落实国家宏观调控的总体部署，进一步转变外汇管理理念和方式，在风险可控的前提下，尽可能为经济主体提供便利，逐步淡化事前审批管理，强化事后监测分析职能。推进外汇管理重点领域改革，加强异常跨境资金流动监管，提高外汇管理政策透明度，完善外汇储备经营管理，促进国际收支平衡。

Abstract

In 2009, due to the massive stimulus policies, the global economy rebounded and showed increasing signs of recovery. The Chinese economy smoothly survived the toughest year in the new century with a stable and upward momentum.

In 2009, influenced by the international financial crisis, balance of payments activities in China generally slowed down, and transactions of major items such as trade in goods, trade in services, and direct investment decreased compared with 2008. The "twin surpluses" were maintained under the current account and the capital and financial account. The situation of the balance of payments (BOP) was improved: the current account surplus to GDP accounted for 6.1 percent, decreasing for two consecutive years by 3.5 percentage points year on year in 2009. Net exports made a negative contribution to China' s economic development whereas domestic demand made a greater contribution. Along with the improved economic performance, net inflows of foreign capital rebounded gradually, and in the second half of 2009, the BOP surplus reached a higher level than that of the first half of the year and growth was positive. In general, the surplus disequilibrium remained a prominent issue.

In 2010, the global economic situation is expected to improve. The developed countries will gradually stabilize and the emerging markets countries will be the main drivers for the global economy. If the Chinese economy maintains stable and rapid development, the macro environment for the balance of payments will improve. Meanwhile, driven by market factors including the exchange rate and the interest rate, cross-border capital flows will tend to be more active and net capital inflows may be even more impressive. Nevertheless, with the implementation of policies for an adjustment of the development strategy and economic structure, the effect of the ratio of the current account surplus to GDP may further decrease and overseas investment by domestic institutions will be kept at reasonable level, thus helping to improve the situation of China's balance of payments.

In the future, adjustments of the development strategy and economic structure will be further emphasized. The foreign exchange administration will fulfill its overall macro–control strategy and further adjust ideas and methodology of foreign exchange administration to aid economic entities, but with the precondition of controlling risks. Prior authorizations will be gradually removed, and monitoring and analysis will be emphasized. The SAFE will promote reforms in major fields of foreign exchange administration, intensify administration of abnormal cross–border capital flows, enhance the transparency of foreign exchange administration, improve foreign exchange reserve management, and promote the situation of the balance of payments.

目录

专栏

图

表

Contents

Boxes

Charts

Tables

一、国际收支概况

（一）国际收支运行环境

2009 年，国际金融危机总体上从恶化蔓延趋向缓和好转，个别性风险事件时有发生，经济金融形势呈现出变化快、波动大、不确定性依然存在等突出特点。

宏观经济总体触底反弹，但复苏基础尚不稳固。2009 年初危机持续恶化蔓延，全球经济全面陷入衰退，市场普遍担心“第二波冲击”。第二季度以来，在政府大力救助和市场自我修复的双重作用下，危机恶化局面得到缓解，全球经济逐步企稳复苏。各国复苏进程出现分化，部分新兴市场国家率先企稳，主要发达国家也陆续在下半年走出经济衰退，但与亚洲等新兴市场国家相比，经济恢复速度较缓。整体复苏基础较为脆弱，复苏的动力主要来自大规模政策刺激下的制造业反弹和存货调整，主要国家的就业形势依然严峻，私人需求尚未有效启动，经济复苏依然面临不确定性。

国际金融市场先抑后扬，市场趋稳过程中频繁震荡。第二季度以来，国际金融市场信心明显恢复，投资者风险偏好有所回升，股市、汇市、商品市场等均由极端水平快速回调：主要股票指数在创下近十年新低后大幅反弹，受危机中避险情绪升温和资金回流等因素持续推高的美元汇率显著回落，国际原油价格波动上涨，黄金价格屡创新高。但从全球范围看，去杠杆化过程仍在持续，信贷增长尚未恢复，市场避险情绪未完全散去，极易受到局部和个别信用事件的影响，金融市场呈现出波动回升的态势。

2009 年，我国国际收支的国内环境经历了较大变化。上半年，受国际金融危机持续扩散蔓延影响，我国经济下行压力明显加大，有效需求不足矛盾凸显；进出口出现负增长，对外贸易形势发生逆转；外资流入势头放缓，甚至出现部分外资撤资情况。下半年，党中央、国务院不断丰富完善应对国际金融危机的一揽子计划和政策措施，我国经济在全球率先回升向好，全年 GDP 增长 8.7%；内需对经济增长的拉动作用显著增强；出口形势逐步好转，利用外资稳步增长，下半年外汇资金净流入势头明显加快。

专栏 1

2009 年主要涉外经济政策调整

2009 年是 21 世纪以来我国涉外经济发展最为困难的一年。面对 2008 年第四季度以来国际金融危机持续扩散蔓延，国家全面实施并不断丰富完善应对国际金融危机的一揽子计划和政策措施，在统筹做好保增长、调结构、惠民生的基础上，对外开放迈出新步伐。主要措施包括：

一是出台稳定外需政策。加快调整加工贸易政策，从限制类目录和禁止类目录中分别剔除1 730个和106个十位商品编码。完善机电产品出口政策，2009年8月以来，先后5次调整机电产品出口退税率，退税率达到17%的机电产品约占机电产品总税号的70%，覆盖了机电产品出口的60%。出台421亿美元大型成套设备出口融资保险专项安排以及优惠出口买方信贷100亿美元。在广东、上海等部分地区开展跨境货物贸易人民币结算试点。完善出口收结汇联网核查制度，提高预收货款和延期付款等基础比例，调增2009年度金融机构短期外债指标用于支持企业贸易融资。

二是转变外贸增长方式，促进贸易平衡。大力实施科技兴贸战略，新增20家科技兴贸创新基地，积极扩大机电和高新技术产品出口，同时着力扩大先进技术设备、关键零部件和重要能源资源进口。修订出台《禁止进口限制进口技术管理办法》、《鼓励进口技术和产品目录》等相关规定和措施，进一步完善技术进出口管理体制。修改完善了《服务贸易发展规划纲要》，制定完善了服务贸易促进政策。加快落实促进服务外包产业发展，在财政、税务、信贷、外汇等管理环节出台多项配套措施，支持20个示范城市开展服务产业外包。大力促进重点领域服务出口，重点支持文化、中医药、软件等领域的服务出口。

三是加强对外资引导，提高利用外资质量。简化审批程序，下放融资租赁、投资性公司等外资企业审批权限。加强对外商投资的引导，出台鼓励外商投资研发中心的税收政策。修订中西部地区外商投资优势产业目录，推动外资向中西部地区转移。加快生态园区建设，增强了开发区的产业集聚功能和节能减排、集约利用资源方面的示范效应。鼓励境外机构投资者进入境内市场开展中长期证券投资，将单家合格境外机构投资者投资额度上限由8亿美元调整至10亿美元，将养老基金、保险基金、开放式中国基金等进行中长期投资的本金锁定期缩短至3个月。

四是支持“走出去”战略。出台《境外投资管理办法》，进一步改善国内企业对外投资环境。发布162个国家和地区的对外投资合作国别（地区）指南，整合建成对外投资合作信息服务系统。鼓励企业在发达国家设立研发中心，支持以获取能源资源、先进技术和营销网络为目标的并购投资。境外直接投资外汇资金来源审核和资金汇出核准调整为登记管理，在汇兑环节上对境外直接投资基本不再限制。允许符合条件的各类国内企业在一定限额内使用自有外汇或人民币购汇等多种方式进行境外放款，支持境内企业对外投资。

五是反对各种形式的贸易保护主义，维护公正合理的贸易投资环境。针对国际金融危机爆发后贸易摩擦明显增多的严峻形势，利用G20金融峰会等各种多边、双边场合，坚决反对贸易保护主义。通过WTO多边平台，妥善处理美国等国玩具进口措施、日本肯定列表制度、欧盟危险化学物质分类等对我国有较大影响的技术性贸易摩擦，维护了我国企业和产业的正当利益。进一步加强贸易救济和反垄断调查，2009年对外发起反倾销调查八起、反补贴调查三起。积极开展经营者集中反垄断审查执法，依照《反垄断法》对可口可乐公司收购汇源公司不予批准，有条件地批准英博啤酒公司收购AB啤酒公司，促进了市场公平竞争。

（二）国际收支主要状况

2009年我国国际收支继续呈现“双顺差”格局。其中，经常项目顺差为2 971亿美元，较2008年下降32%，2008年为增长17%；资本和金融项目顺差为1 448亿美元，较2008年增长6.6倍，2008年为下降74%。各主要项目情况如下：

1. 货物贸易进出口多年来首次回落

2009年，由于外部需求依然较低，国内经济增速相对前些年有所回落，我国货物贸易进出口继续呈现下滑趋势。按国际收支统计口径，2009年货物贸易出口为12 038亿美元，进口为9 543亿美元，分别较2008年下降16%和11%，是近20年来的首次下降；货物贸易顺差为2 495亿美元，下降31%。

2. 服务贸易逆差持续增长

2009年，服务贸易收入为1 295亿美元，较上年下降12%；支出为1 589亿美元，与2008年基本持平；逆差为294亿美元，增长149%。服务贸易逆差扩大的主要原因是，运输项目逆差较2008年扩大93%，旅游项目由2008年的顺差47亿美元转为逆差40亿美元。

3. 收益项目净流入小幅上升

2009年收益项目顺差为433亿美元，较2008年增长4%，增幅回落57个百分点。随着我国对外资产规模的进一步扩大，2009 年投资收益流入 994 亿美元，增长 7%，其中大部分是国家外汇储备取得的收益。在全球经济不景气的情况下，我国海外务工人员的劳务收入增幅放缓，2009 年职工报酬净流入为 72 亿美元，较 2008 年增长 12%，增幅回落 35 个百分点。

4. 直接投资顺差减少

2009 年，直接投资顺差为 343 亿美元，较 2008 年下降 64%。由于国际资本流动规模收缩，外国来华直接投资净流入为 782 亿美元，较 2008 年下降 47%。我国对外直接投资保持一定规模，2009 年净流出为 439 亿美元，较 2008 年下降 18%。

5. 证券投资净流入略有下降

2009 年，证券投资项下净流入为 387 亿美元，较 2008 年下降 9%。其中，我国对外证券投资净回流为 99 亿美元，较 2008 年下降 70%；境外对我国证券投资净流入为 288 亿美元，增长 191%。

6. 其他投资由净流出转为净流入

2009 年，贷款、贸易信贷、货币和存款等形式的其他投资项下净流入为 679 亿美元，2008 年为净流出 1 211 亿美元。其中，我国境外其他投资资产净回流为 94 亿美元，2008 年为净流出 1 061 亿美元。境外对我国其他投资净流入为 585 亿美元，2008 年为净流出 150 亿美元。

7. 储备资产增幅放缓

2009 年，剔除汇率、价格等非交易价值变动（即估值效应）影响，我国新增国际储备资产 3 984 亿美元，按可比口径较 2008 年减少 17%。其中，外汇储备交易变动为 3 821 亿美元，特别提款权和货币黄金合计增加 160 亿美元。

专栏 2

国际收支平衡表中外汇储备记录方法的调整

外汇储备资产的存量变动包括两个部分，一是由于国际收支交易引起的外汇储备的变动，包括因持有外汇资产带来的收益，简称交易变动；二是由于价格、汇率等非交易因素引起的价值变动，简称非交易价值变动（即估值效应）。按照《国际收支统计手册》（第五版）的定义，国际收支平衡表中外汇储备资产记录的应是交易变动；而国际投资头寸表中记录的外汇储备存量，既包含交易变动，也包含非交易变动。目前，国际上大多数国家按照这一标准编制国际收支平衡表和国际投资头寸表。

自1996年起，国家外汇管理局按照国际货币基金组织《国际收支手册》（第五版）统计原则编制国际收支平衡表，中国国际收支平衡表中经常项目以及资本和金融项目的统计基本遵循《国际收支手册》（第五版）的原则，但历年平衡表中外汇储备资产的统计是个例外。以往，该数据来自人民银行，为各年末外汇储备资产余额相减的结果，该结果既包含当期外汇储备交易变动，也包括外汇储备存量的非交易变动。虽然该储备资产的记录方法不完全符合国际收支平衡表应只记录交易数据的原则，但由于往年汇率、价格等非交易因素变动较小，其所引起的储备资产的变动相对较少，因此，该记录方法对合理判断以往年度的国际收支状况不会造成重大影响。

2008年以来，由于我国外汇储备资产规模增长较快，且国际市场美元汇率波动较大，外汇储备资产中非交易变动规模日益扩大，可能影响社会对真实国际收支状况的判断。在此情况下，国家外汇管理局决定从编制2009年年度平衡表开始，按照国际惯例对平衡表中外汇储备资产记录方法进行调整，即从以往记录外汇储备年度余额变动数据，调整为仅记录外汇储备资产交易变动数据，剔除非交易变动的影响。以2009年为例，年末外汇储备资产余额为23 992亿美元，较上年末增加4 531亿美元。其中由于交易净增的3 821亿美元记入平衡表外汇储备资产变动，另有710亿美元外汇储备资产变动是由汇率、价格等非交易因素引起的，不再记入平衡表，而将在2009年末国际投资头寸表中反映。

将非交易因素引起的外汇储备资产变动从平衡表外汇储备资产中剔除，既符合国际收支平衡表统计的国际惯例，也便于数据使用者更好地分析平衡表各项目的关联关系，减少将非交易数据纳入相关分析带来的问题。

表 1–1　2009 年中国国际收支平衡表①　　单位：亿美元

项　目	差　额	贷　方	借　方
一、经常项目	**2 971**	**14 846**	**11 874**
A. 货物和服务	**2 201**	**13 333**	**11 132**
a. 货物	**2 495**	**12 038**	**9 543**
b. 服务	**−294**	**1 295**	**1 589**
1. 运输	−230	236	466
2. 旅游	−40	397	437
3. 通讯服务	0	12	12
4. 建筑服务	36	95	59
5. 保险服务	−97	16	113
6. 金融服务	−3	4	7
7. 计算机和信息服务	33	65	32
8. 专有权利使用费和特许费	−106	4	111
9. 咨询	52	186	134
10. 广告、宣传	4	23	20
11. 电影、音像	−2	1	3
12. 其他商业服务	59	247	188
13. 别处未提及的政府服务	1	9	8
B. 收益	**433**	**1 086**	**653**
1. 职工报酬	72	92	21
2. 投资收益	361	994	632
C. 经常转移	**337**	**426**	**89**
1. 各级政府	−2	0	3
2. 其他部门	340	426	86
二、资本和金融项目	**1 448**	**7 464**	**6 016**
A. 资本项目	**40**	**42**	**2**
B. 金融项目	**1 409**	**7 422**	**6 014**
1. 直接投资	**343**	**1 142**	**799**
1.1 我国对外直接投资	−439	42	481
1.2 外国来华直接投资	782	1 100	318
2. 证券投资	**387**	**981**	**594**
2.1 资产	99	669	570
2.1.1 股本证券	−338	122	461
2.1.2 债务证券	437	547	110
2.1.2.1（中）长期债券	370	479	110
2.1.2.2 货币市场工具	67	68	0
2.2 负债	288	312	24
2.2.1 股本证券	282	288	7
2.2.2 债务证券	6	23	17

① 我国国际收支平衡表按国际货币基金组织《国际收支手册》（第五版）规定的各项原则编制，采用复式记账原则记录所有发生在我国内地居民（不包括港、澳、台地区）与非居民之间的经济交易。本表计数采用四舍五入原则。

续表

项　目	差　额	贷　方	借　方
2.2.2.1(中)长期债券	6	23	17
2.2.2.2 货币市场工具	0	0	0
3. 其他投资	**679**	**5 299**	**4 620**
3.1 资产	94	1 174	1 080
3.1.1 贸易信贷	−544	0	544
长期	−38	0	38
短期	−506	0	506
3.1.2 贷款	130	450	320
长期	−315	0	315
短期	445	450	5
3.1.3 货币和存款	52	267	216
3.1.4 其他资产	456	457	1
长期	0	0	0
短期	456	457	1
3.2 负债	585	4 125	3 540
3.2.1 贸易信贷	321	321	0
长期	22	22	0
短期	298	298	0
3.2.2 贷款	37	3 222	3 185
长期	−97	135	232
短期	134	3 087	2 953
3.2.3 货币和存款	116	456	340
3.2.4 其他负债	111	126	15
长期	110	110	0
短期	1	16	15
三、储备资产	**−3 984**	**0**	**3 984**
3.1 货币黄金	−49	0	49
3.2 特别提款权	−111	0	111
3.3 在基金组织的储备头寸	−4	0	4
3.4 外汇	−3 821	0	3 821
3.5 其他债权	0	0	0
四、净误差与遗漏	**−435**	**0**	**435**

（三）国际收支运行评价

2009 年，国际金融危机影响仍然存在，我国国际收支交易活动总体上放缓。我国国际收支交易总规模为 4 万亿美元，较 2008 年下降 12%；与同期 GDP 之比为 81.9%，较 2008 年下降 18.9 个百分点。各主要交易项目收支规模较 2008 年有所回落。按国际收支统计口径，货物贸易总额为 21 581 亿美元，下降 14%；服务贸易总额为 2 885 亿美元，下降 6%；外国来华直接投资流入为 1 100 亿美元，下降 32%；

对外直接投资流出为 481 亿美元，下降 14%。

图 1-1

中国国际收支交易规模及其占 GDP 比例

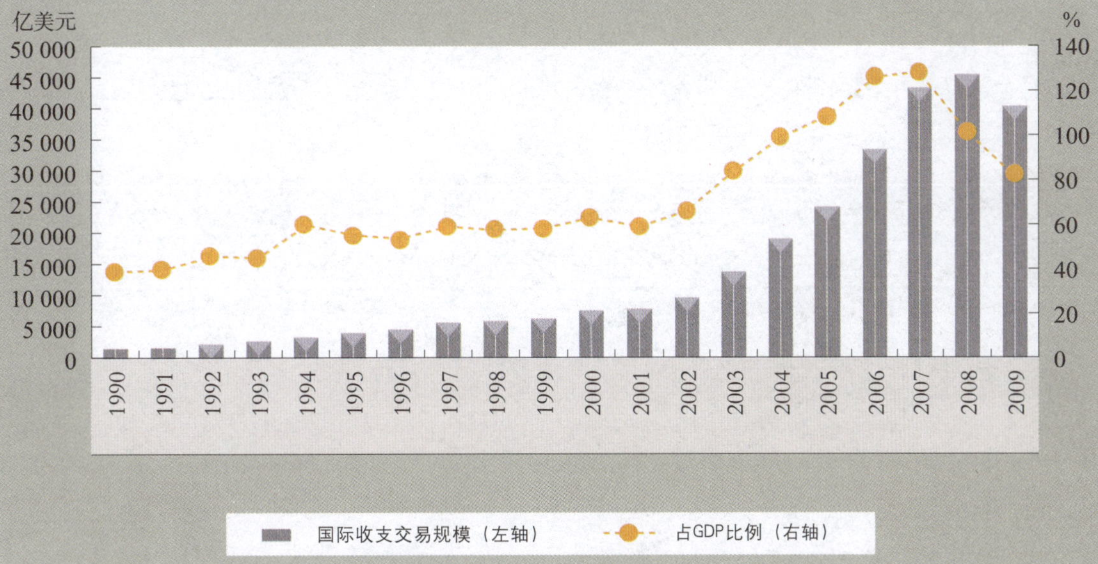

我国国际收支保持“双顺差”格局，国际收支状况继续改善。2009 年国际收支总顺差为 4 420 亿美元，较 2008 年下降 3%，2008 年比 2007 年增长 2%。经常项目顺差与同期 GDP 之比为 6.1%，较 2008 年下降 3.5 个百分点，连续第二年呈回落态势。外需对我国经济增长的拉动作用为负，对内需的贡献力度加大。

表 1-2　2003—2009 年国际收支顺差结构　　单位：亿美元

项　目	2003 年	2004 年	2005 年	2006 年	2007 年	2008 年	2009 年
国际收支总顺差	986	1 794	2 238	2 599	4 453	4 551	4 420
经常项目差额	459	687	1 608	2 533	3 718	4 361	2 921
占 GDP 比例	2.8%	3.6%	7.2%	9.5%	11.0%	9.6%	6.1%
资本和金融项目差额	527	1 107	630	67	735	190	1 448
占 GDP 比例	3.2%	5.8%	2.8%	0.3%	2.2%	0.4%	3.0%

随着国内外宏观经济环境的改变，国际收支运行起伏加大。2009 年上半年，在国际金融危机的冲击下，国际收支交易总规模较 2008 年同期下降 27%，其中，货物贸易、服务贸易总额分别下降 24% 和 14%，6 月末外债余额较 2008 年末小幅下降 4%。下半年，国内外经济企稳向好势头明显，国际收支交易总规模超过上半年，同比增长 6%，其中，货物贸易总额同比下降 5%，服务贸易总额同比增长 2%，

2009年末外债余额较6月末上升19%。

外汇资金净流入规模逐步恢复，国际收支失衡问题依然突出。2009年第二季度以来，外汇净流入触底回升，国际收支逆转风险趋于缓解。上半年，国际收支总顺差为1 955亿美元，较2008年同期下降26%；下半年，国际收支总顺差为2 465亿美元，较2008年同期增长29%。从主要交易项目看，下半年货物贸易、收益和经常转移顺差均高于上半年，外国来华直接投资净流入是上半年的1.7倍。总体上，2007年至2009年国际收支总顺差持续超过4 000亿美元，处于历史上的较高水平。

图 1–2

中国国际收支经常项目差额及其占 GDP 比例

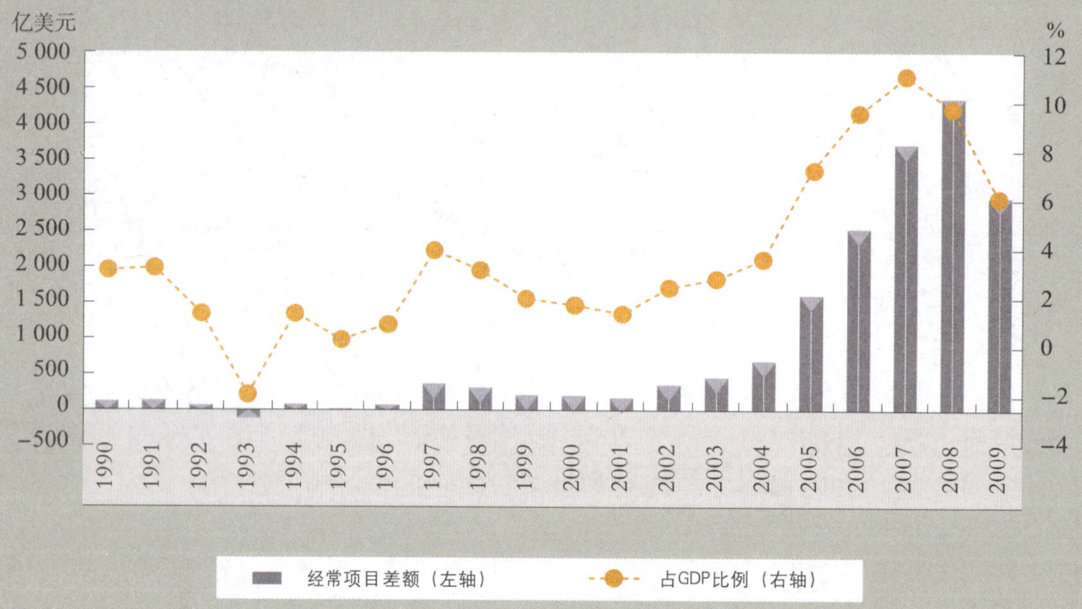

专栏 3

我国异常跨境资金流动特点

当前，经济全球化和金融自由化快速发展，金融产品日趋丰富，金融交易更加便利，资本在全球配置和逐利已成为普遍现象。随着我国经济对外开放程度的不断提高，跨境资金流动规模成倍扩大，2009年通过国家外汇管理局国际收支统计监测系统申报的跨境收入和支出接近3 200万笔，国际收支交易规模达到3.6万亿美元，在正常的贸易投资活动中难免夹杂着部分异常跨境资金流动。同时，我国经济市场化程度不断深化，银行、企业、个人等市场主体的市场意识逐渐增强，对价格信号的变化更加明显，以规避风险或套取收益为动机的交易行为有所增多。近年来，我国经济在世界范围内表现突出，人民币汇率出现一定程度的升值预期，国内外利率水平也存在差异，为一些套利资金提供了运作的空间，部分异常跨境资金流出入不可避免。

目前，我国的异常跨境资金流动在特征表现上不同于新兴经济体的“热钱”。一是主要通过合法合规的渠道流动。由于我国对跨境资本和金融交易仍有一定管制，异常跨境资金往往通过经常项目、直接投资、银行自营和个人等非管制渠道流动，而不会通过证券投资、外债等短期资本项目实现。二是大部分以长期投资方式存续。在我国经济长期高增长的前景下，人民币汇差、利差存在长期的套利空间，异常跨境资金一般不会快进快出，而是更加注重长远收益。三是许多套利资金的操作主体是境内机构。例如，国内商业银行通过调回境外资产发放国内外汇贷款，获取国内更高的利息收益；境内机构通过境外上市或设立特殊目的公司融资，将境外资金引入境内运用。四是一些资金流入发挥了支持企业发展的作用。目前我国投融资体制有待完善，许多企业尤其是中小民营企业融资较难，部分资金需要通过体制外民间融资（包括境外融资）解决，这在一定程度上弥补了国内投融资体制的不足，但需要规范和引导。

总体来看，对异常跨境资金流动需要加强监测和分析，坚持疏堵并举、标本兼治，制定有针对性的政策措施，通过外汇、商务、海关、税务、工商、金融监管等部门联合监管，提高防控能力。

二、国际收支主要项目分析

(一) 货物贸易

2009 年，我国货物贸易总体呈现下降走势。按国际收支统计口径，货物贸易进出口总值为 21 581 亿美元，同比减少 14%。其中，出口为 12 038 亿美元，减少 16%；进口为 9 543 亿美元，减少 11%；货物贸易顺差为 2 495 亿美元，减少 31%。据海关统计，2009 年我国货物贸易呈现以下主要特点：

贸易顺差明显下降，进口降幅小于出口。2009 年进出口总额为 22 072 亿美元，较 2008 年下降 14%，其中：出口额为 12 017 亿美元，下降 16%；进口额为 10 056 亿美元，下降 11%，进口降幅低于出口降幅 5 个百分点。全年货物贸易顺差为 1 961 亿美元，下降 34%，净减少 1 020 亿美元。自 2008 年 10 月起进出口连续数月下挫后，2009 年 3 月货物贸易开始企稳，但仍未恢复到危机前的水平。

一般贸易出现逆差，加工贸易顺差降低。2009 年，我国一般贸易进出口总额为 10 637 亿美元，较 2008 年下降 14%，其中：出口额为 5 298 亿美元，下降 20%，降幅高于总体出口；进口额为 5 339 亿美元，下降 7%，降幅低于总体进口；出口降幅大于进口降幅 13 个百分点，一般贸易由 2008 年顺差 899 亿美元转为逆差 41 亿美元。我国加工贸易进出口总额为 9 093 亿美元，下降 14%，其中：出口额为 5 870 亿美元，下降 13%；进口额为 3 223 亿美元，下降 15%。加工贸易顺差 2 647 亿美元，下降 11%。

图 2-1

改革开放以来中国进出口总值及其变动情况

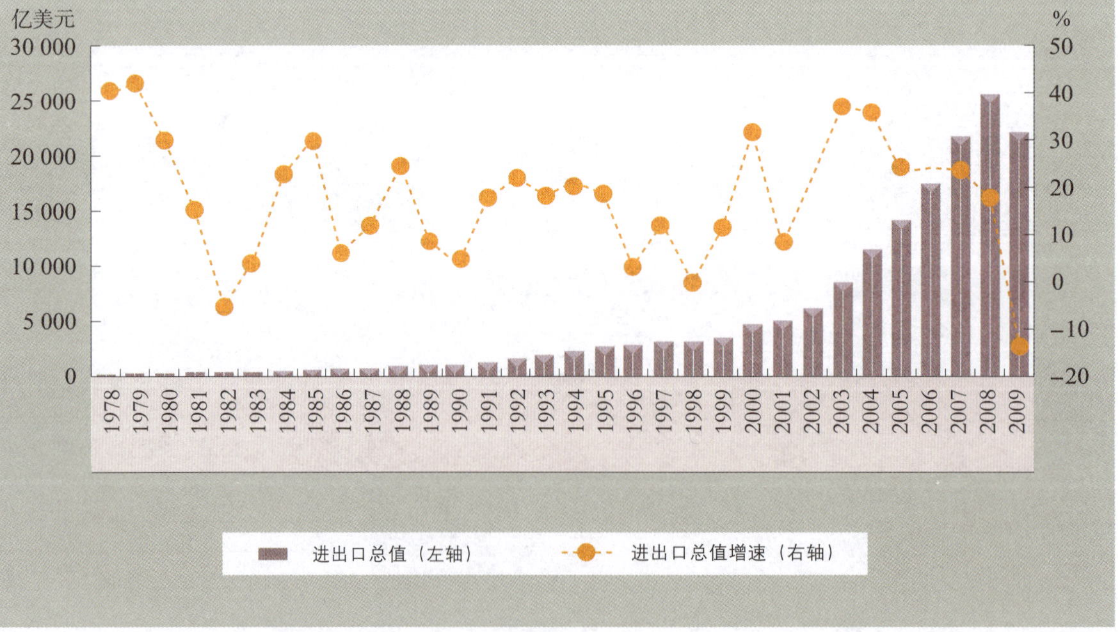

外商投资企业顺差降幅小于总体降幅，国有企业逆差扩大，民营企业进口增长。2009 年，外商投资企业进出口规模变化与总体相当，其中，出口额为 6 722 亿美元，下降 15%；进口额为 5 452 亿美元，下降 12%；顺差 1 270 亿美元，下降 26%，低于总体贸易顺差降幅 8 个百分点。国有企业进出口规模受金融危机影响更大，出口额为 1 910 亿美元，下降 26%，高于总体出口降幅 10 个百分点；进口额为 2 885 亿美元，下降 19%，高于总体进口降幅 8 个百分点；逆差 975 亿美元，净增加 9 亿美元。民营企业出口额为 3 384 亿美元，下降 12%；进口额为 1 719 亿美元，增长 8%；顺差 1 665 亿美元，减少 549 亿美元。

来自欧美市场的进口降幅较小，与周边国家或地区贸易保持逆差。2009 年，欧盟仍为我国第一大贸易伙伴，中欧双边贸易总值为 3 640 亿美元，下降 15%，其中，进口仅下降 3.7%；我国对欧盟顺差 1 085 亿美元，下降 32%。位居第二位的中美双边贸易总值为 2 983 亿美元，下降 11%，其中，进口仅下降 4.8%；我国对美国贸易顺差 1 434 亿美元，下降 16%。在前十大贸易伙伴中，我国与日本、东盟、韩国、中国台湾、澳大利亚和巴西间均为贸易逆差。

初级产品进口量保持增长，劳动密集型产品出口降幅较小，贸易条件重现恶化趋势。2009 年，我国初级产品进口量基本保持增长，其中：铁矿砂进口 6 亿吨，增长 42%；原油进口 2 亿吨，增长 14%；煤进口 1.3 亿吨，增长 2.1 倍；铜进口 429 万吨，增长 63%；粮食进口 207 万吨，增长 27%。我国机电产品和高新技术产品进口分别为 4 914 亿美元和 3 098 亿美元，均下降 9%。劳动密集型产品出口同比降幅小于总体出口降幅，其中，服装出口额为 1 071 亿美元，下降 11%；纺织品出口额为 600 亿美元，下降 8%；鞋类出口额为 280 亿美元，下降 6%。机电产品和高新技术产品出口额为 7 131 亿美元和 3 769 亿美元，分别下降 13%和 9%。尽管 2009 年我国贸易条件较 2008 年改善 8.7%，但我国出口商品结构和定价机制没有根本变化，国际大宗商品价格逐步回升，贸易条件在 2008 年末至 2009 年初短暂好转之后又重新恶化，2009 年 12 月贸易条件指数较 2 月下降 14%。

（二）服务贸易

2009 年，我国服务贸易收入为 1 295 亿美元，较 2008 年下降 12%，服务贸易支出为 1 589 亿美元，与 2008 年持平；逆差 294 亿美元，较 2008 年上升 149%。我国服务贸易呈现以下主要特点：

服务贸易总额降幅小于货物贸易，我国对外贸易结构有所改善。2009 年，服务贸易总额为 2 885 亿美元，下降 6%，低于货物贸易总额降幅 8 个百分点。在服务贸易收支整体出现下降的情况下，仍有部分服务贸易项目收入或支出出现增长。2009

年，我国在建筑、金融、旅游项目支出继续增长，增速均超过 20%；在别处未提及的政府服务、金融和保险项目收入保持增长，增速均超过 15%。

服务贸易逆差迅速扩大说明当前我国服务贸易整体上仍缺乏比较优势。服务贸易逆差较 2008 年增长 1.49 倍，逆差主要来自运输、专有权利使用费和特许费、保险及旅游项目，逆差分别为 230 亿美元、106 亿美元、97 亿美元和 40 亿美元。其中，旅游项目自 1982 年以来在年度平衡表中首次出现逆差。旅游收入为 397 亿美元，减少 3%；旅游支出为 437 亿美元，增长 21%；逆差为 40 亿美元，2008 年同期为顺差 47 亿美元。2009 年，受世界经济不景气的影响，我国入境人数较上年明显减少。而支出方面，随着国民收入水平的进一步提高，我国居民消费结构呈现多元化发展态势，消费导向不仅局限于货物贸易范畴，服务贸易所占比重逐步增长，因私出境旅游支出不断扩大，2009 年我国出境人数增长 4%。从分国别旅游收入和支出测算的情况看，我国对美国、中国澳门和澳大利亚均呈较大幅度的逆差。

图 2-2

中国对主要国家和地区的旅游收支情况

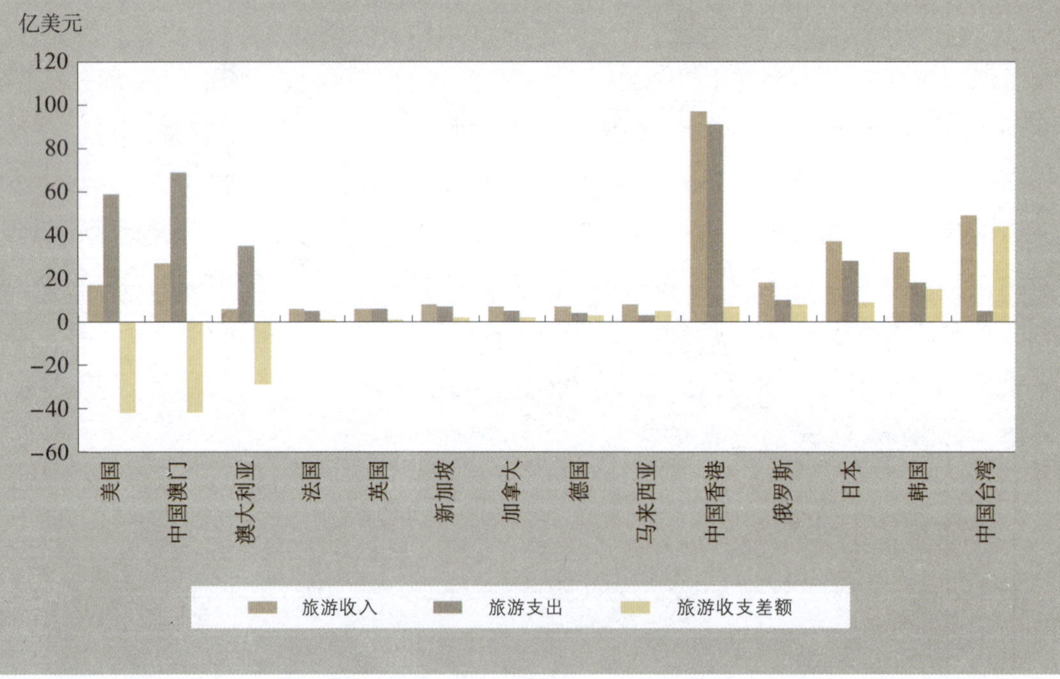

呈现顺差的服务贸易项目有所减少。在 13 个服务贸易项目中，2009 年有 6 项呈现顺差，主要为其他商业服务、咨询、建筑以及计算机和信息服务项目，顺差分别为 59 亿美元、52 亿美元、36 亿美元和 33 亿美元。2008 年有 8 项呈现顺差，其

中旅游、电影音像和通讯服务两个顺差项目在2009年转为逆差。

运输和旅游仍是我国服务贸易的主要项目，但比重略有下降。2009年运输和旅游收入分别占服务贸易总收入的18%和31%，支出分别占服务贸易总支出的29%和27%。两项目收支合计占服务贸易总规模的53%，比重较上年下降约1个百分点。与此同时，建筑服务、专有权利使用费和特许费、计算机和信息服务收支规模占比略有上升。

服务贸易主要伙伴国家和地区基本保持稳定，集中度较高。服务贸易收支前十名伙伴国家和地区占全部服务贸易收支的78%。其中，服务贸易收入来源国家和地区排名前五位的是中国香港、美国、日本、新加坡和韩国，支出目的国家和地区排名前五位的仍是中国香港、美国、日本、韩国和中国澳门。

专栏4

我国个人外汇业务的特点和变化

近年来，随着我国涉外经济的迅猛发展，个人外汇收支（即个人资金跨境收付）和结售汇（即个人资金本外币转换）规模不断扩大。为支持和便利个人合理依法持有与使用外汇，提高个人外汇管理和服务水平，国家外汇管理局不断完善个人外汇管理政策。目前，个人结汇和境内个人购汇实行每人每年等值5万美元的年度总额管理。在年度总额内，本人凭有效身份证件直接在银行办理，基本可以满足个人日常的用汇需求。

当前，我国个人外汇收支及结售汇形成了以下特点：一是业务主体规模庞大，办理外汇收支和结售汇业务的个人既包括我国公民，也包括来我国的外国人。二是业务种类多样，个人跨境外汇收支和结售汇业务在经常项目、资本和金融项目中均有所体现。三是国际、国内经济金融形势及汇率变动对个人外汇收支和结售汇活动具有显著影响，同时季节性因素也对个人外汇业务发生作用。

我国个人外汇收支规模总体呈扩大趋势，个人外汇支出增长较快[①]。2006—2009年，个人外汇收支总额年均增长11%，其中，个人外汇收入年均增长3%，个人外汇支出年均增长45%。近年来，随着我国个人出境留学、旅游的增多，个人外汇支出一直呈较快增长态势。在此影响下，2006—2009

① 数据来源：国际收支统计监测系统。

年个人外汇收支顺差年均下降13%，其中2009年个人外汇收支顺差402亿美元，较上年下降41%。

个人结售汇变动趋势与个人外汇收支情况相同，个人购汇明显提升[①]。

图 2-3

2006—2009年个人外汇收支情况

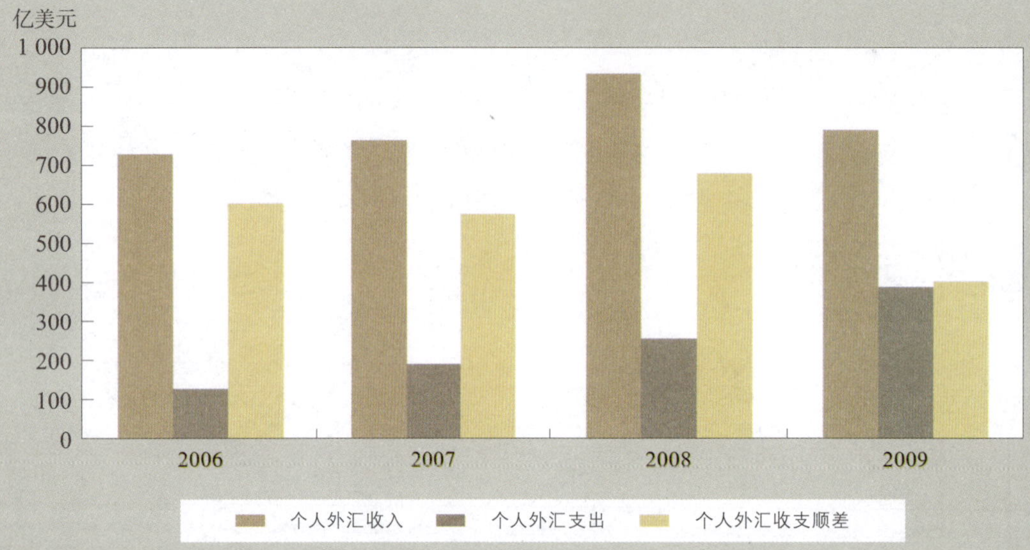

图 2-4

2006—2009年个人结售汇情况

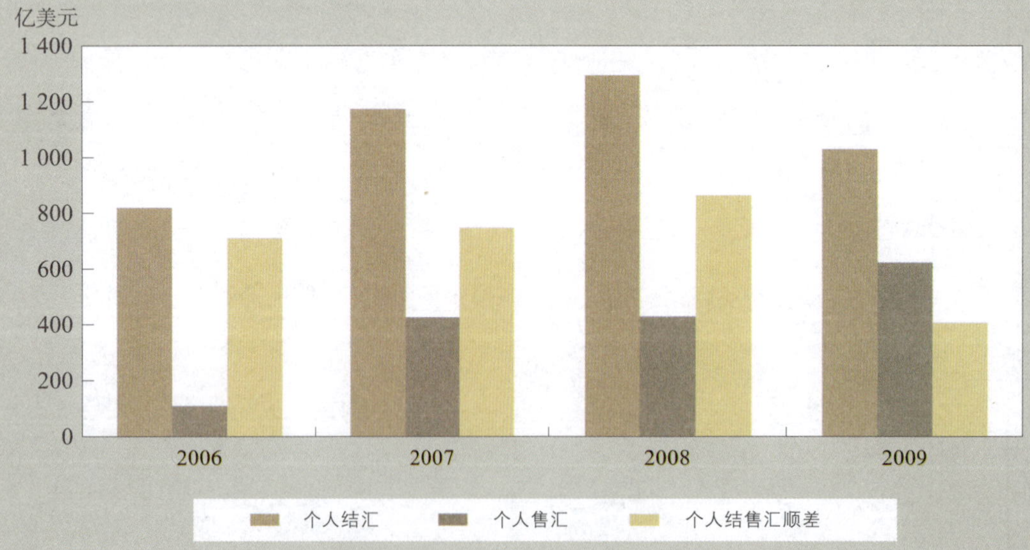

① 数据来源：银行结售汇统计系统。

2006—2009 年，个人结售汇总额年均增长 21%，其中，个人结汇年均增长 8%，个人购汇年均增长 79%。2009 年个人结汇较上年下降 20%，购汇增长 45%，结售汇顺差 407 亿美元，下降 53%。

（三）直接投资

1. 外国来华直接投资下降

按国际收支统计口径，2009 年外国来华直接投资流入 1 100 亿美元，较 2008 年下降 32%；撤资清算等流出 318 亿美元，增长 143%，增幅比 2008 年增加 126 个百分点；净流入 782 亿美元，下降 47%[①]。2009 年外国来华直接投资的主要特点是：

金融和非金融部门吸收外国来华直接投资均呈现下降态势。金融部门吸收外国来华直接投资 41 亿美元，下降 72%；非金融部门吸收外国来华直接投资 1 059 亿美元，下降 28%。

图 2-5

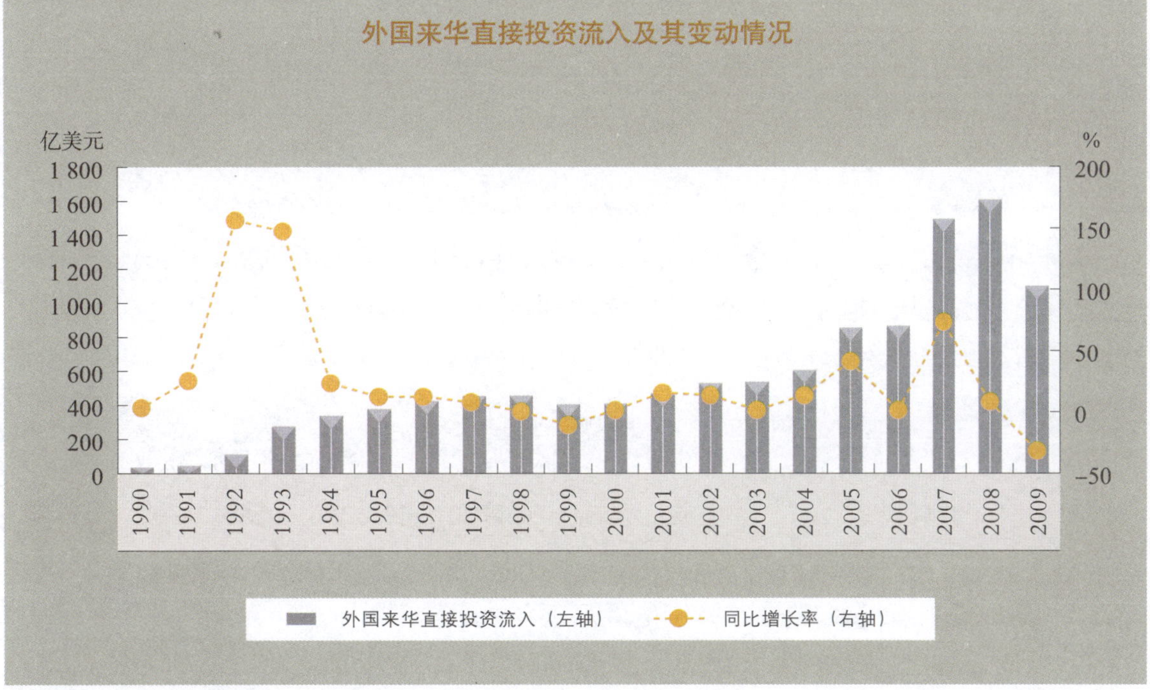

数据来源：国际收支平衡表。

① 国际收支统计口径的外国来华直接投资流入（贷方）为在我国设立外商投资企业的投资，包括股本金、收益再投资和其他资本；流出（借方）包括外商投资企业撤资和清算资金的流出。目前，由于受统计时点、统计口径以及统计质量等方面的影响，与商务部公布的实际利用外资数据存在一定差异。

非金融部门外国来华直接投资的资金来源地较为集中。2009 年，外国来华直接投资资金来源前十位国家和地区依次为：中国香港、美国、新加坡、日本、中国台湾、英属维尔京群岛、韩国、德国、法国和英国，前十位国家和地区在华投资金额占外国来华直接投资总额的 91%。

各行业的外国来华直接投资呈现不同特点。水利、环境和公共设施管理业，金融业，租赁和商务服务业，建筑业和农、林、牧、渔业受到外资青睐，投资增长较快，分别增长了 123%、49%、19%、12% 和 11%。居民服务和其他服务业、采矿业、制造业和房地产业的实际利用外资资金下降较快，分别下降了 54%、54%、31% 和 30%。其他行业的外国来华直接投资均有不同程度的下降。

外国来华直接投资的撤资清算以及外方股东贷款的流出较大。由于美国银行等境外银行减持境内银行的股权投资 104 亿美元（占外国来华直接投资流出的 33%），导致 2009 年外国来华直接投资撤资清算资金的大幅增长。剔除该因素的影响，外国来华直接投资撤资清算 212 亿美元，增长 62%，主要为非金融部门的外方股东贷款的流出。

2. 对外直接投资减少

2009 年，我国对外直接投资 481 亿美元，较 2008 年下降 14%；对外直接投资撤资清算等汇回 42 亿美元，增长 91%；净流出 439 亿美元，下降 18%。2009 年我国对外直接投资的主要特点是：

金融和非金融部门对外直接投资呈现不同的态势。金融部门对外直接投资 47 亿美元，下降 69%；非金融部门对外直接投资 434 亿美元，增长 7%。

从投资目的地看，我国金融部门对外投资主要集中在中国香港、英国、美国等金融市场较为发达的地区。非金融部门对外直接投资集中在亚洲和拉丁美洲。其中，对亚洲地区的投资占非金融部门对外直接投资总额的 59%，对拉丁美洲地区的投资占 25%，对其他地区的投资占 16%。

从投资的行业分布看，我国非金融部门对外直接投资涉及商务服务业（即以投资控股为主要目的的投资）、采矿业、批发和零售业、制造业、交通运输业、房地产业等众多领域。其中，商务服务业和采矿业是对外直接投资的主要行业，分别占非金融部门对外直接投资总额的 55% 和 25%。

从投资方式看，2009 年我国非金融部门对外直接投资以收购方式为主，占投资总额的 40%。

（四）证券投资

2009 年，我国证券投资净流入为 387 亿美元，比 2008 年下降 9%。其中，我国对外证券投资净回流为 99 亿美元，下降 70%；境外对我国证券投资净流入为 288 亿美元，上升 1.91 倍。

1. 对外股本证券投资大增，债券投资继续回流

对外股本和债券证券投资大出大进。其中，对外股本证券投资净流出为 338 亿美元，2008 年为净流出 11 亿美元；对外债券证券投资净流入为 437 亿美元，上升 29%。这主要是因为境内不同部门外资资产配置发生变化。一方面，境内非银行机构正在成为对外股本证券投资的主力，对外股权投资迅速扩大，外汇资产投资转向积极；另一方面，境内商业银行仍是对外债券证券投资的主体，因国际金融市场风险依然较大，同时国内企业对外汇贷款的需求大增，商业银行减持对外债券类资产。2009 年，在商业银行吸收的外汇存款新增 162 亿美元的情况下，国内外汇贷款增加 1 045 亿美元。

2. 境外对我国证券投资净流入增加

2009 年，境外证券投资净流入为 288 亿美元。其中，股本证券投资净流入为 282 亿美元，债务证券投资净流入为 6 亿美元。股本证券投资净流入主要为我国企业赴境外上市筹资以及境外机构购买美国银行出售的部分中国建设银行境外上市股票[①]。此外，合格境外机构投资者（QFII）对我国投资也有所增长，2009 年净流入为 33 亿美元。债务证券投资净流入较 2008 年下降 46%，主要是由于偿还外债本金增长快于新借外债增长。

专栏 5

银行部门外汇资产境内外配置变动的影响

2009 年，我国国际收支资本和金融项目顺差为 1 448 亿美元，同比增长 6.6 倍，其中，证券投资顺差为 387 亿美元，其他投资顺差为 679 亿美元。银行部门将大量境外证券投资和同业拆放资产调回境内运用是我国资本和金融项目顺差较快增长的重要原因。

① 根据国际货币基金组织《国际收支手册》统计原则，当非居民持有居民机构 10%或以上有投票权的股权时，视为非居民对居民机构的直接投资。当非居民持股比例低于 10%，视为非居民对居民机构的证券投资。根据这一统计原则，美国银行减持中国建设银行股权，以及其他非居民随后获得这些股权，一方面，记录为我国机构吸收外国来华直接投资的减少；另一方面，对应记录为非居民对中国证券投资的增加。

在国际金融危机背景下，银行境外资产运作面临较大风险且收益逐步下降。随着美国量化宽松货币政策的实施，伦敦同业拆借市场一年期美元利率由2009年初的1.9%左右降至12月末的1%左右，而国内一年期美元贷款加权平均利率2009年初为3%，12月为1.9%，高于境外同业拆借利率1个百分点。

在这种情况下，2009年我国银行部门减少境外资产663亿美元，其中，减持境外（中）长期债券442亿美元，减少境外贷款（主要为同业拆放）129亿美元，减少境外货币和存款（主要为同业存放）92亿美元，占减持境外资产的比例分别为67%、19%和14%。同期，银行部门境外证券投资和其他投资负债增加121亿美元。综上所述，银行部门境外资金净流入为784亿美元，占证券投资和其他投资顺差的74%，占资本和金融项目顺差的54%。

银行大量调回的境外资金成为其发放国内外汇贷款的重要来源。2009年我国金融机构国内外汇贷款增加1 045亿美元，银行境外资金调回相当于国内外汇贷款增加额的七成多。一方面，银行调回大量资金便利了企业借用外汇贷款支付进口或对外投资，从而替代了购汇，增加了净结汇的压力。从2009年第二季度起，银行代客结售汇顺差重新大于银行代客跨境收支顺差，改变了2008年7月后净结汇小于净流入的局面。从结汇和售汇情况分别来看，结汇规模逐季回升，但结汇率（银行代客结汇／跨境外汇收入）没有明显变化，而售汇规模增长较慢，售汇率（银行代客售汇／跨境外汇支出）明显下降。外汇资金购汇流出意愿降低是结售汇顺差扩大的主要原因。另一方面，银行大量减少境外资产也大大提高了银行的外汇贷存比和外汇资产负债期限错配风险。一旦美元利率和汇率重新走高，境内外汇贷款需求下降，银行有可能重新增加外汇资产的境外配置，导致外汇流出和国际收支顺差的下降。

（五）外债

截至2009年末，我国外债余额为4 286亿美元，较2008年末增长10%。其中，登记外债余额为2 669亿美元，同比增长2%；贸易信贷余额为1 617亿美元①，同比上升25%。

---

① 2009年贸易信贷抽样调查方法进行了调整，按新方法统计余额为1 617亿美元。为保证数据的可比性，2008年末贸易信贷余额由按原方法统计的1 141亿美元相应调整为1 296亿美元。

按期限划分，中长期外债（剩余期限）余额为 1 694 亿美元，占外债余额的 40%；短期外债（剩余期限）余额为 2 593 亿美元，占外债余额的 60%。

图 2–6

中国外债余额及短期外债（剩余期限）占比

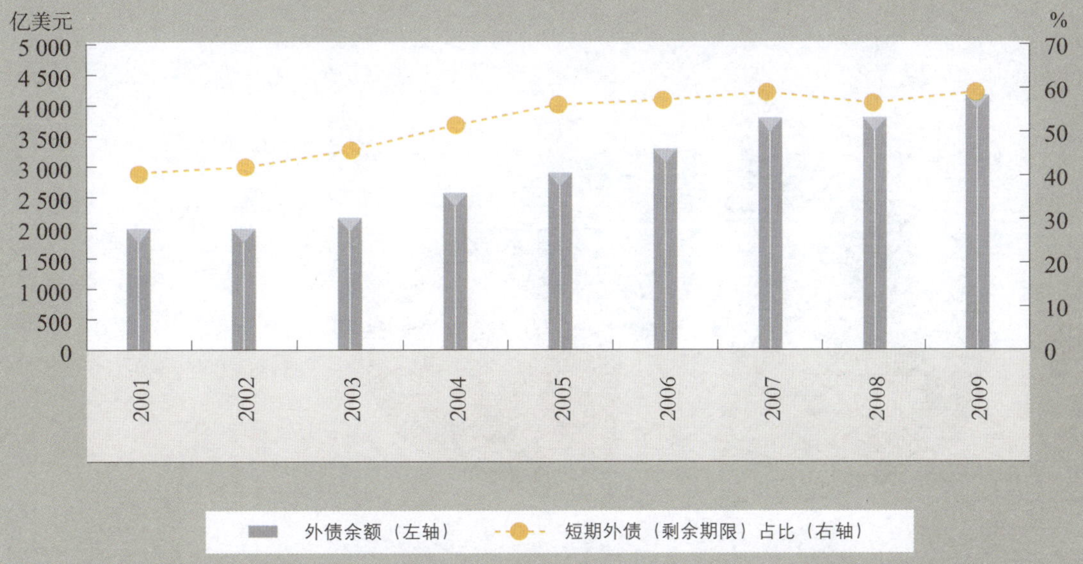

从债务类型看，以国际商业贷款为主。2009 年末，国际商业贷款余额为 1 986 亿美元，占登记外债余额的 74%，所占比重较 2008 年末下降 3 个百分点。

图 2–7

中国登记外债债务类型结构

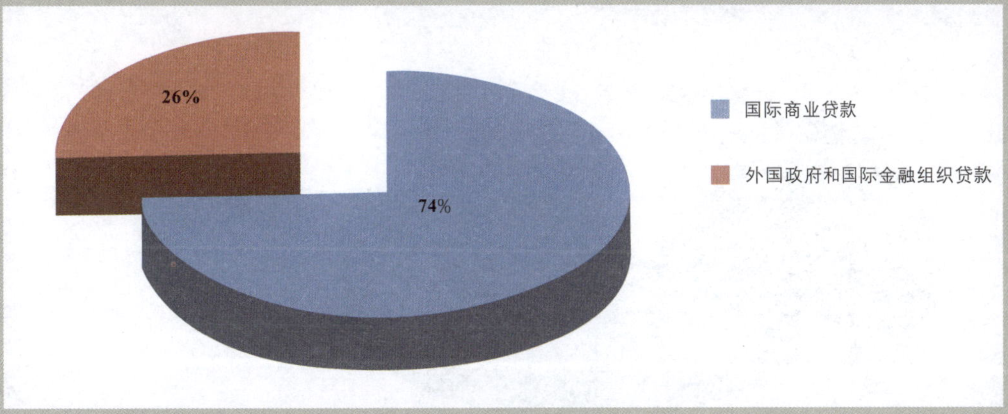

从债务主体看，以中资金融机构和外资企业为主。在2009年末的登记外债余额中，中资金融机构和外商投资企业债务余额分别为941亿美元和932亿美元，均占35%。

图 2-8

中国登记外债债务主体结构

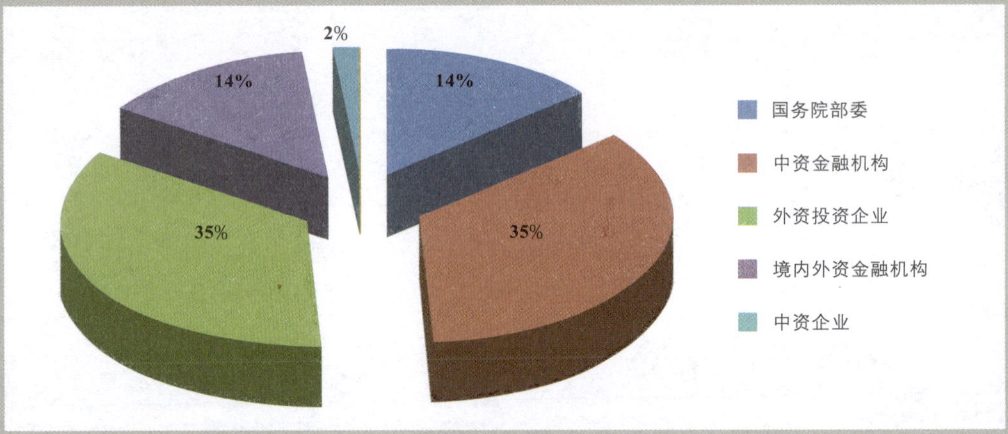

从币种结构看，以美元债务为主。在2009年末的登记外债余额中，美元债务占68%，比2008年末下降0.5个百分点；其次是日元债务，占12%，比2008年末上升0.1个百分点。

图 2-9

中国登记外债币种结构

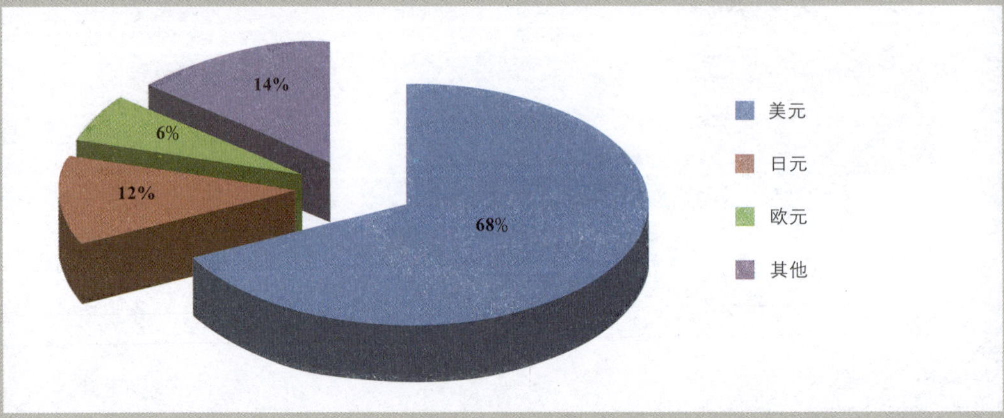

中长期债务主要投向制造业及交通运输、仓储和邮政业等基础设施建设。按照国民经济行业分类，在登记的 1 881 亿美元中长期外债（签约期限）余额中，投向制造业的为 391 亿美元，占 21%；投向交通运输、仓储和邮政业的为 238 亿美元，占 13%。

图 2–10

中国中长期外债（签约期限）投向结构

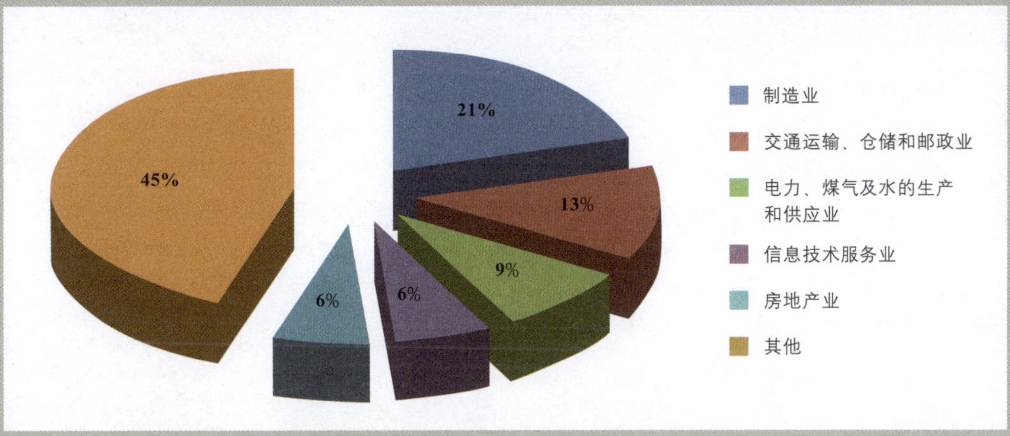

2009 年，我国外债变动呈现以下特点：

全年外债总规模先抑后扬。2009 年第一季度外债余额继续延续 2008 年第四季度的下降态势，第二至第三季度较 2008 年末小幅上扬，第四季度则大幅上升，主要源自贸易信贷的增加和中资金融机构远期信用证及海外代付项下对外债务增加。第一至第四季度外债余额季环比分别增长 –1.1%、5.6%、–0.6% 和 5.9%，其中：贸易信贷外债余额季环比分别增长 2.7%、17.5%、–3.6% 和 7.3%；中资金融机构外债余额季环比分别增长 –5.0%、5.5%、4.8% 和 8.1%。

外债总规模回升的主要推动因素是贸易信贷和中资金融机构外债余额增加。按可比口径计算，2009 年末，我国外债余额比上年末增加 385 亿美元。其中，贸易信贷余额较 2008 年末增加 321 亿美元，对外债余额增长的贡献率为 83%；中资金融机构外债余额增加 113 亿美元，对外债余额增长的贡献率为 29%，二者合计对外债余额增长的贡献率达 112%。

三、外汇市场运行与人民币汇率

（一）银行间外汇市场改革和建设情况

1. 扩大外汇市场交易主体，丰富外汇市场主体层次

截至2009年末，银行间即期外汇市场会员总数达到276家，远期、外汇掉期和货币掉期会员分别为73家、71家和20家，除货币掉期会员数与2008年末持平外，其他三类会员分别增加8家、4家和2家。企业集团财务公司等非银行金融机构类会员继续扩大，全年新增7家。

2. 上线新一代外汇交易系统，进一步提升外汇市场运行效率

2009年4月27日，中国外汇交易中心新一代外汇交易系统三期正式上线，进一步升级系统功能和用户界面，并引入新的订单交易策略，使交易系统的功能更趋多样化、操作更趋人性化。新系统上线后，运行保持稳定，交易效率提升，市场反映良好。

3. 实施询价交易净额清算，降低外汇市场运行成本与风险

2009年6月1日，银行间外汇市场即期询价交易净额清算正式推出，国内外汇市场开始实施以多边净额清算为基础的清算对手方制度，有利于降低外汇交易的信用风险和清算风险，夯实对系统性风险的防范能力，促进外汇市场特别是衍生产品市场的长远发展。

4. 丰富外汇市场交易平台，促进外汇市场公平竞争

3家货币经纪公司获准开展外汇经纪业务，进一步提高了外汇市场流动性和交易效率。同时，规范中国外汇交易中心对银行间外汇市场衍生产品交易人工服务收费，促进中国外汇交易中心与货币经纪公司之间形成互补互动和公平竞争的有序市场环境。

（二）人民币对主要货币汇率走势

1. 人民币对美元汇率保持基本稳定

2009年末，人民币对美元汇率中间价收于6.8282元/美元，较2008年末（6.8346）升值64个基点。

图 3-1

图 3-2

注：年初中间价 =100。

2. 人民币对其他主要货币有升有贬

2009年，人民币对港币汇率中间价期末收于0.88048元/港元，较2008年末的0.88189元/港元升值0.2%。人民币对日元汇率中间价期末收于7.3782元/100日元，较2008年末的7.5650元/100日元升值2.5%。人民币对欧元汇率中间价期末收于9.7971元/欧元，较2008年末的9.6590元/欧元贬值1.4%。人民币对英镑汇率中间价期末收于10.9780元/英镑，较2008年末的9.8798元/英镑贬值10.0%。

3. 银行间外汇市场交易价弹性下降

2009年，银行间即期外汇市场人民币对美元交易价围绕中间价窄幅波动，交易价相对中间价的日间最大波幅日均为0.04%，2008年为0.15%；交易价的日间波幅（最高价—最低价）日均为29个基点，较2008年下降82个基点。

4. 境内外人民币汇率预期由贬转升

2009年，境内外远期市场人民币对美元汇率整体呈现先贬后升走势，下半年人

图 3-3

2009年境内外远期市场1年期人民币对美元汇率走势

民币升值预期明显增强。第一季度，美元保持远期升水，人民币存在一定程度的贬值预期，其中境外 NDF 的一年期美元最大升水幅度超过 2 500 个基点，人民币预期贬值幅度接近 4%，而同期境内远期市场的美元升水幅度远低于境外市场。3 月下旬以后，受国际市场美元转为弱势的影响，境内外远期市场人民币开始走强，境外 NDF 从 4 月开始转为人民币升值预期，而境内远期市场人民币贬值和升值预期交替出现。9 月下旬以来，国内经济持续向好，推动境内远期市场人民币也转为升值预期，并延续至年末，境内外一年期人民币预期升值幅度一度分别接近 2.5% 和 4%。

5. 人民币有效汇率波动较大

2009 年以来，受人民币对美元汇率中间价保持基本稳定的影响，人民币有效汇率（即多边汇率）追随国际市场美元汇率的走势，呈现先升后贬走势。根据国际清算银行（BIS）的数据，2009 年前 3 个月，人民币名义有效汇率指数持续升值，累计升值 4.1%，此后连续 8 个月走贬，至 12 月人民币名义有效汇率指数为 111.68，较 2008 年末贬值 5.4%，较汇改前（2005 年 6 月）累计升值 12.7%，较国际金融危机全面爆发前的 2008 年 6 月累计升值 3.3%。扣除通货膨胀差异后的人民币实际有

图 3–4

1994 年 1 月至 2009 年 12 月人民币有效汇率走势

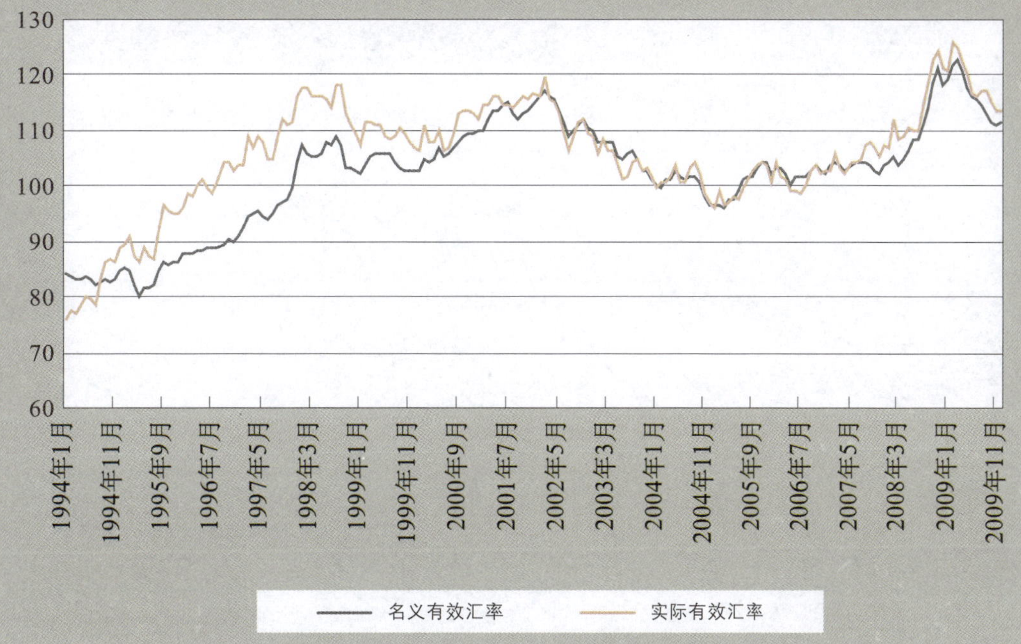

效汇率指数也呈现类似走势，前2个月累计升值4.0%，此后连续5个月走贬，8月小幅反弹后再次走贬，至12月人民币实际有效汇率指数为113.78，较2008年末贬值6.1%，较汇改前（2005年6月）累计升值16.3%，2008年6月以来累计升值3.4%。

（三）银行间外汇市场交易

1. 银行间即期外汇交易

随着全球金融市场的逐步趋稳以及国内银行间外汇市场询价交易净额清算的推出，2009年市场交易止跌回升，已恢复并超过2008年国际金融危机发生前的水平。全年银行间即期外汇市场成交量较2008年增长19.3%，日均成交量增长20.3%。即期外汇市场仍以询价交易为主，全年询价与竞价交易量之比为249∶1。

2. 银行间远期外汇交易

2009年，银行间远期外汇市场累计交易2 501笔，成交97.67亿美元，日均成交0.40亿美元，总成交量和日均成交量较2008年分别下降43.8%和43.3%。

图 3–5

2007 年 1 月至 2009 年 12 月银行间市场远期和外汇掉期成交量

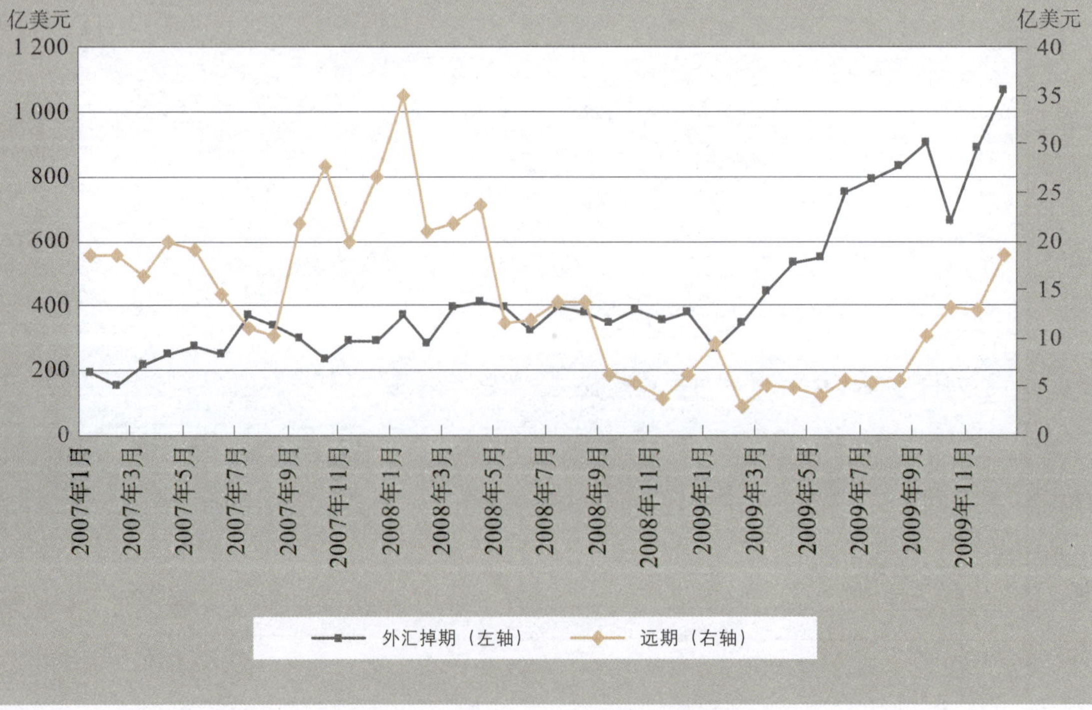

3. 银行间外汇掉期交易

2009 年，银行间外汇掉期累计交易 30 708 笔，成交 8 018.02 亿美元，日均成交量为 32.86 亿美元，总成交量和日均成交量较 2008 年分别增长 82.1% 和 83.6%。

4. 银行间外币对外币买卖

截至 2009 年末，银行间外币买卖市场共有做市商银行 16 家，会员银行 84 家。全年 8 个外币对即期买卖累计成交 31 620 笔，累计成交量折合 347.86 亿美元，日均成交 1.43 亿美元，较 2008 年减少 43.3%。

表 3–1　2009 年银行间外币买卖市场各外币对交易情况

货币对	欧元 / 美元	澳元 / 美元	英镑 / 美元	美元 / 日元	美元 / 加元	美元 / 瑞士法郎	美元 / 港元	欧元 / 日元
成交量（亿美元）	98.77	8.88	29.30	23.40	11.74	3.46	168.94	3.38
成交量占比（%）	28.4	2.6	8.4	6.7	3.4	1.0	48.6	1.0
成交量同比增长（%）	−59.4	80.9	−8.3	−69.2	−22.5	−18.4	−29.1	−50.2
笔数	14 648	2 099	2 786	4 585	720	332	5 683	767

注：成交量为折美元金额。

5. 外汇市场的流动性和效率提高

2009 年，做市商制度对维护市场流动性继续发挥积极作用，做市商交易规模稳步增长，全年交易量增速略高于整个市场的增长，市场份额为 90.2%，较 2008 年上升 2.7 个百分点。在电子报价系统的支持下，2009 年做市商对交易请求的响应速度继续提高，并且双边有效报价点差最小降至 2.7 个基点，全部做市商平均值为 4.2 个基点，较 2008 年下降 6.4 个基点。

四、国际收支形势展望和政策取向

（一）形势展望

从国际看，2010年世界经济形势预计继续稳定向好，新兴市场国家将成为全球经济增长的主要动力，发达国家经济也将止跌回稳。各国大规模刺激政策措施及其相互协调日益加强，有利于全球范围内的信心恢复，国际间双向资金流动可能加快，金融市场交易趋于活跃，金融体系的系统性风险继续下降。国际货币基金组织（IMF）2010年1月预测，2010年全球经济增长为3.9%，将超过2008年的增长水平。同时，危机的后续影响将广泛而持久地显现，国际经济金融稳定仍面临诸多挑战。高企的失业率、庞大的财政赤字和政府债务、救助政策退出的不确定性、贸易和投资保护主义抬头等危机的后续影响交互作用，可能导致尚不稳固的经济基本面受到冲击和震荡。金融体系尚未根本企稳，信贷扩张的恢复和金融机构资产负债表的修复仍待时日，在政府救助动力消减的情况下，仍需密切关注个别大型机构可能爆发的非系统性风险。美国、欧元区等发达经济体复苏前景存在差异，欧元区部分国家财政赤字较大、融资能力较低、主权债务风险加大，可能影响全球经济金融的稳定。

从国内看，2010年我国经济将保持较快增长，依然成为全球经济复苏中的一大亮点。国家着力加快经济发展方式转变和经济结构调整，内需对经济增长的作用将更加突出。一方面，国家继续实施积极的财政政策，政府在民生领域的投资资金将保持一定规模。在适度宽松的货币政策下，随着经济活动的日益活跃，以及相关措施的更加便利，民间投资的积极性有望提高。另一方面，国家扩大居民消费需求的力度将进一步加大。调整国民收入分配格局、完善社会保障机制、促进城乡消费增长等政策措施继续发挥一定作用，有利于国内消费水平的提升。但我国经济仍存在一些突出矛盾和问题，国际经济金融环境的不确定性因素仍然较多，国内经济发展方式转变、经济结构调整的难度较大，管理通胀预期、稳定物价总水平的任务也比较突出。

综上所述，2010年国内外经济环境总体趋向稳定，我国国际收支交易将更加活跃。国际收支总规模增速可能快于国内经济增长，国际收支总规模与GDP的比例在2008年、2009年下滑后，2010年有可能恢复增长。同时，2010年我国国际收支顺差规模仍会较大。我国经济率先复苏，国内投资机会较多，劳动力等要素价格仍具有竞争优势，跨国公司来华直接投资流入将有所扩大，而国内利率水平相对较高，人民币升值预期有所增强，也会增加跨境资金套利交易规模。但我国促进国际收支平衡的基础也正在进一步得到夯实，2010年国际收支状况有望继续改善。贸易顺差扩大态势将继续缓解，经常项目顺差与GDP的比例可能进一步下降。随着我国企业对外投资步伐的加快，资本流出也会增加。从中长期看，国家推动经济发展方式转变和经济结构调整的大政方针，将为国际收支平衡创造基本条件。

专栏 6

后危机时期的风险事件

2009 年以来，在各国大规模刺激政策的推动下，全球经济和金融体系自 3 月份起逐步摆脱了国际金融危机的严峻局面，呈现企稳复苏的积极景象。与此同时，局部和个别风险事件仍时有发生，不仅涉及实体经济信用风险，还涉及主权风险，相关国家乃至全球的经济复苏和金融稳定进程受到影响。

美国汽车业财务危机：2009 年初，随着国际金融危机不断深化，并向实体经济扩散蔓延，私人消费大幅下滑，汽车市场急剧萎缩，汽车业融资渠道受阻，美国大型汽车制造商现金流纷纷告急，亟须重组。通用、福特和克莱斯勒汽车陷入财务危机，美国政府通过提供资金援助、购车优惠等措施救助三大汽车公司，但成效有限。2009 年中，克莱斯勒、通用汽车分别通过快速破产程序完成重组，其中克莱斯勒将优质资产出售给由全美汽车工会、菲亚特以及美国、加拿大政府组成的集团，通用汽车将优质资产出售给由美国政府持股 60.8%的新通用汽车公司。

迪拜世界集团违约：受金融危机冲击，迪拜房地产、旅游、贸易、金融等支柱产业均陷入困境，导致依赖高债务杠杆发展、背负 590 亿美元高额债务的迪拜最大国有企业——迪拜世界集团（Dubai World）资金链断裂，于 2009 年 11 月宣布，其与下属子公司 Nakheel 全部债务的偿还期限将延至 2010 年 5 月 30 日以后，并要求债权人同意其停止偿付此前到期债务。随着阿布扎比政府和阿联酋中央银行出台相关救助政策，以及集团与其债权人债务重组谈判的推进，违约事件对全球特别是新兴市场的震荡影响逐步减弱。截至 2010 年 2 月初，迪拜政府已向迪拜世界集团注资 62 亿美元。

希腊主权评级降级事件：2009 年底，由于希腊财政赤字高企、政府债务负担较重，且政府未能采取有效措施应对，希腊主权评级遭到惠誉、标普、穆迪三家评级机构的下调，成为欧元区国家中首个被评级机构降至 A- 级以下的国家。降级事件大幅拉宽了希腊主权债利差，并加剧市场参与者对欧元区内同样面临高赤字、高债务、低增长、银行体系状况较差等问题的国家主权风险的担忧，评级机构接连对爱尔兰、西班牙、葡萄牙等国采取了负面评级行动，上述三国主权债利差大幅攀升。市场普遍担心欧元区国家主权风险的上升，可能引发连锁反应，拖累区内经济复苏的步伐。

此外，冰岛总统否决英荷储户存款赔偿法案，亚洲最大航空公司日本航空、美国最大的中小企业商贷机构CIT集团破产重组等风险事件也对经济金融市场产生了不同程度的影响。

后危机时期的风险事件警示，在全球经济金融逐渐摆脱严峻局面的过程中，危机的后续影响将广泛而持久地显现，实体经济和金融市场仍存在相当风险和不确定性，特别是债务负担较重的国家、地区和发行体仍有可能发生违约或受到冲击，经济金融的个别和局部风险仍需密切关注。

（二）政策取向

2010年，外汇管理工作将全面贯彻落实国家宏观调控的总体部署，服务于发展方式转变和经济结构调整的战略目标，进一步转变外汇管理的理念和方式，推进外汇管理重点领域改革，在风险可控的前提下，将尽可能为经济主体提供便利，逐步淡化事前审批管理，强化事后监测分析职能。下一阶段，外汇管理部门将重点加强异常跨境资金流动监管，提高外汇管理政策透明度，完善外汇储备经营管理，促进国际收支平衡。具体包括：

一是推进外汇管理重点领域改革。进一步推进进出口核销、外汇账户、拓宽资本流出渠道等重点领域和关键环节改革，规范国内外汇市场发展，促进涉外经济平稳较快发展。二是进一步完善异常跨境资金流动监管。构建完善的监测预警、非现场检查和应急管理体系，完善贸易信贷、服务贸易以及对外担保等外汇管理，对地下钱庄等外汇违法违规行为开展专项打击行动。丰富外汇管理政策工具，防范和化解跨境资本流动风险。三是进一步提高外汇管理政策透明度。推进《国际收支统计申报办法》的修订工作，拓宽国际收支统计数据的发布范围。加大外汇管理法规的整合力度，加强与媒体和公众的沟通交流，及时就社会关注的外汇管理热点问题做好宣传解释。四是进一步完善外汇储备经营管理机制，努力实现外汇储备资产安全和保值增值。

I . Overview of the Balance of Payments

(I) The Balance of Payments Environment

In 2009, rather than continuing to deteriorate the international financial crisis was alleviated. Certain risks did occur from time to time, but the overall economic and financial situation was characterized by rapid changes, considerable fluctuations, and sustained uncertainties.

The macro economy rebounded, but at the beginning of the year, the crisis continued to deteriorate. The global economy slumped into a recession and worries about a "second shock" prevailed in the market. Since the second quarter, the deteriorating crisis was relieved owing to both the governments' crisis bailout measures and the self-healing of the market, and the global economy gradually stabilized. In the meantime, countries recovered at different paces: whereas some emerging markets countries took the lead in stabilizing, the major developed countries successively reduced the recession in the second half of the year, but with a slower growth rate than that in the emerging markets countries of Asia. In general, the foundation for a recovery was still weak because the main drivers came from manufacturing and inventory adjustments due to the massive stimulus policies, the employment situation was still serious, private demand had not effectively taken off, and the global economy was still facing uncertainties.

The international financial market followed an upward trend after its former downward trend, with frequent fluctuations as it stabilized. Since the second quarter, international financial markets have recovered with increased confidence, the propensity for investment resumed and the stock markets, foreign exchange market, and commodity markets recovered from their extremely low levels. The main stock market indices rebounded from their new ten-year low, the USD exchange rate experienced a significant drop from its high level due to enhanced risk aversion and capital inflows, the price of crude oil appreciated amidst fluctuations, and the price of gold recorded repeated new highs. However, with the persistence of the deleveraging process, credit growth did not recover and with the existence of a propensity for risk aversion, the financial markets showed an upward trend amidst fluctuations due to particular credit events.

In 2009, the domestic economic environment for China's balance of payments experienced considerable changes. In the first half of the year, influenced by the sustained extension of the international financial crisis, the Chinese economy was challenged by ever-increasing downward pressures and increased conflicts between effective supply and demand. Import and export growth was negative, leading to a reversal in foreign trade performance. Foreign capital inflows slowed down and some foreign capital was divested. In the second half of the year, the Central Committee and the State Council continued to enrich the package of measures to deal with the crisis, and the Chinese economy took the lead in recovering, with an annual GDP growth of 8.7 percent. Domestic demand significantly promoted economic growth. The export situation gradually recovered, foreign capital utilization grew steadily, and the momentum for net inflows of foreign capital grew.

Box I

Adjustments in the External Economic Policies in 2009

With respect to China's external economic development, 2009 was the most difficulty year since the beginning of the 21st century. Challenged by the sustained extension of the international financial crisis since the last quarter of 2008, the country launched and continually enriched a package of plans and measures to deal with the crisis and took new steps in the reform and opening based on a sound foundation for sustaining economic growth, adjusting the economic structure, and improving the livelihood of the people. The main policies include:

First, stabilizing external demand. Policies regarding processing trade were adjusted by eliminating 1 730 and 106 codes from the list of prohibited commodities and restricted commodities respectively. Since August 2009, Export policies regarding machinery and electronic products were improved by adjusting rebate rates on five occasions, and products with a rebate rate of 17 percent accounted for 70 percent of the total duty items and 60 percent of the total exports. Export credit insurance totaling USD 42.1 billion was specifically allocated for exports of complete set of equipment. A pilot program for RMB settlement of cross-border trade in goods was carried out in Guangdong and Shanghai. The administration of online inspections for the collection and settlement of foreign exchange for exports was improved by increasing the quota for advance receipts and deferred payments. The annual short-term external debt quota for financial institutions in 2009 was increased in order to support trade financing for enterprises.

Second, adjusting the development of foreign trade to promote a trade equilibrium. The strategy of supporting foreign trade through technology was launched by establishing 20 innovation bases for trade that boosted science and technology, increasing exports of machinery and electronic products and high-tech products, and managing to increase imports of high-tech equipment, key components, and important energy and resource items. Related measures regarding regulations for the administration of import prohibitions and restrictions of technology and the catalogue of preferential imports of technology and products were amended to further improve regulation of technology imports and exports. The trade in services development plan was amended to improve regulation of development of trade in services. The development of the outsourcing services industry was encouraged by many supportive measures in fiscal, tax, credit, and foreign exchange administrative policies and by supporting outsourcing services in 20 model cities. Exports of services were promoted by supporting the export of cultural items, traditional Chinese herbs, and software.

Third, improving the quality of foreign capital by strengthening guidance of foreign capital. The approval procedures were simplified by decentralizing approval authority for financing of leasing and investment companies by foreign enterprises. Guidance over foreign capital was strengthened by launching a tax policy to encourage a foreign-funded research and development center. The Catalogue of Priority Industries for Foreign Investment in the Central-Western Regions was amended to facilitate foreign capital transfers to the central-western regions. The construction of a bio-zone was accelerated by strengthening the demonstrative effect of the development zones in industrial agglomeration, energy savings and emission reductions, and intensive utilization of resources. Foreign institutional investors were encouraged to make medium, long-term portfolio investments by adjusting their upper limit from USD 0.8 billion to USD 1 billion and shortening the principal lock-up period of pension funds, insurance funds, and Chinese open-ended funds to 3 months.

Fourth, supporting the going-global strategy. The Administrative Measure for Overseas Investments was implemented to improve the environment for overseas investment by domestic enterprises. The Guidelines for Overseas Investments and Cooperation with Other Countries and Regions with respect to 162 countries and regions were published so as to integrate and establish a cooperative information system for overseas investment.

Enterprises were encouraged to establish research and development centers in the advanced countries and to engage in M&A investments aiming at energy resources, advanced technology, and acquisition of market networks. Prior examinations of the sources of foreign exchange funds for overseas direct investments and authorizations of foreign exchange outward remittances for overseas direct investments were replaced by registration, thus eliminating any restrictions on exchange and remittances for overseas direct investments. Qualified domestic enterprises may extend offshore lending with their own foreign exchange or foreign exchange purchased with RMB within a certain limit to support overseas investment.

Fifth, rejecting all forms of trade protectionism to protect a fair and rational trade and investment environment. Facing the serious situation of increased trade frictions since the onset of the international financial crisis, the country firmly rejected trade protectionism in bilateral and multilateral platforms such as the G20 summit. The government coped with some serious technical trade frictions, such as the toy import regulations by countries including the United States, the positive list system in Japan, and the dangerous chemical substance labels by the European Union, to protect the rightful interests of Chinese enterprises and industries. Trade remedies and investigations into monopolies were further strengthened. In 2009, the Chinese government launched investigations of 8 cases of antidumping and 3 countervailing cases. The authorities actively carried out an anti-monopoly review of concentrated undertakings, denied Coca Cola's application to acquire Huiyuan according to the Anti-Monopoly Law, and approved the acquisition of AB Beer Company by Inbev so as to encourage competition.

(II) Main Characteristics of the Balance of Payments

In 2009, China's balance of payments continued to post twin surpluses. In particular, the current account posted a surplus of USD 297.1 billion, a decrease of 32 percent from year 2008, and the account had increased 17 percent year on year in 2008; the capital and financial account surplus totaled USD 144.8 billion, which increased 6.6 times of that in 2008, whereas the surplus in the capital and financial account decreased 74 percent in 2008. The main items are characterized by the following:

1. The trade surplus in goods decreased for the first time in many years

In 2009, due to low external demand and the slowing down of domestic economic development compared to previous years, imports and exports of Chinese goods followed a decreasing trend. Based on the balance of payments statistics, in 2009, goods exports totaled USD 1 203.8 billion and goods imports totaled USD 954.3 billion, a decrease of 16 percent and 11 percent respectively year on year, representing a decline of each for the first time in 20 years; the trade surplus in goods amounted to USD 249.5 billion, representing a decrease of 31 percent year on year.

2. The deficit in services grew continuously

In 2009, gross revenue from services decreased 12 percent year on year to USD 129.5 billion; payments for services totaled USD 158.9 billion, almost the same level as that in 2008; the deficit in services totaled USD 29.4 billion, an increase of 149 percent year on year. There were two main reasons for this: the increased deficit in transportation that grew by 93 percent year on year and the deficit in travel amounting to USD 4 billion (a surplus of USD 4.7 billion).

3. Net inflows under the income item increased slightly

In 2009, the income item posted a surplus of USD 43.3 billion, an increase of 4 percent year on year and a decline of 57 percentage points with respect to the growth rate. Along with China's further increases in foreign assets, investment income inflows totaled USD 99.4 billion, an increase of 7 percent, among which most came from investment in foreign exchange reserves. Influenced by the global recession, growth of employment compensation slowed down, recording a net inflow of USD 7.2 billion, a decrease of 12 percent year on year and a deceleration of 35 percentage points from the previous year.

4. The surplus in direct investment decreased

In 2009, the surplus in direct investment totaled USD 34.3 billion, a decline of 64 percent year on year. Because of the contraction of international capital flows, foreign direct investment recorded a net inflow of USD 78.2 billion, down 47 percent from the previous year. China's overseas direct investment registered a net outflow of USD 43.9 billion, a decrease of 18 percent year on year.

5. Net inflows of portfolio investment declined slightly

In 2009, net inflows of portfolio investment amounted to USD 38.7 billion, down 9 percent year on year. In particular, outward portfolio investment recorded a net inflow of USD 9.9 billion, down 70 percent year on year; inward portfolio investment totaled USD 28.8 billion, an increase of 191 percent.

6. Other investment recorded a net inflow from earlier net outflows

In 2009, other investment, including loans, trade credits, currency, and deposits, recorded a net inflow of USD 67.9 billion, whereas in 2008 there was a net outflow of USD 121.1 billion. In particular, assets in other investment posted a net inflow of USD 9.4 billion, whereas in 2008 they recorded a net outflow of USD 106.1 billion. Inward other investment recorded a net inflow of USD 58.5 billion, whereas in 2008 there was a net outflow of USD 15 billion.

7. Growth in the accumulation of foreign exchange reserves slowed down

In 2009, due to the revaluation that eliminated non-transactional valuations such as exchange rates and prices, China's international reserves assets increased by USD 398.4 billion, a decrease of 17 percent year on year on a comparative basis, among which foreign exchange reserve transactions and SDR and currency and gold increased by USD 382.1 billion and USD 16 billion respectively.

Box Ⅱ

The Methodology for Recording Adjustments in Foreign Exchange Reserves in the BOP Statistics

There are two constituent parts of stock changes in foreign exchange reserves: one is the change induced by balance of payments transactions, including the income from holding foreign exchange assets, which is called a transactional change, and the other is valuation changes caused by non-transactional factors such as price and exchange rates, which are called non-transactional value changes (revaluation). According to the definition of the BMP5, the BOP records transaction changes of foreign exchange reserves and the IIP records outstanding foreign exchange reserves, which includes not only transactional changes but also non–transactional changes. Today, most countries follow this rule to compile their BOP and IIP.

Since 1996, the State Administration of Foreign Exchange has compiled the country's BOP following the BPM5 methodology of the IMF. Although the current account and capital and financial account statistics follow the BPM5 rules, the recording of foreign exchange reserve assets is an an exception. In the past, the data, on the difference of the outstanding at the beginning and the end of the period came from the People's Bank of China. The data included not only transactional changes but also non–transactional changes. Although the methodology did not fully follow the rule that the BOP only record transaction changes, the asset changes were relatively small, so it did not have a significant effect in China's BOP statement, because in the past non–transaction factors such as the exchange rate and prices changed only slightly.

From 2008, because China's foreign exchange reserve assets accumulated rapidly and the USD exchange rate in international markets fluctuated greatly, the non–transaction changes became more significant, likely having an effect on China's real BOP situation. Under such circumstances, the SAFE decided to adjust its recording methodology for foreign exchange reserves in the BOP according to international conventions, that is, only to record transaction changes and to eliminate non–transaction changes instead of outstanding changes as in the past. For example, outstanding foreign exchange reserves by the end of 2009 totaled USD 2 399.2 billion, representing an increase of USD 453.1 billion, among which transaction changes amounting to USD 382.1 billion were recorded as a foreign exchange reserves change in the BOP, and the other USD 71 billion was due to non–transaction changes, including exchange rates and prices, which was recorded in the 2009 IIP instead of the BOP.

BOP compilation subject to international conventions for BOP compilation helps data users better analyze relations among the different items in the BOP by eliminating from the BOP statistics foreign exchange asset changes caused by non–transaction factors and thus alleviating the problem caused by non–transaction data.

Table 1-1 China's Balance of Payments Statement in 2009①

Unit: USD million

Item	Balance	Credit	Debit
I. Current accounts	**297 142**	**1 484 573**	**1 187 431**
A. Goods and services	**220 112**	**1 333 346**	**1 113 234**
a. Goods	**249 509**	**1 203 797**	**954 287**
b. Services	**−29 398**	**129 549**	**158 947**
1.Transportation	−23 005	23 569	46 574
2.Travel	−4 027	39 675	43 702
3.Communication services	−11	1 198	1 210
4.Construction services	3 595	9 463	5 868
5. Insurance services	−9 713	1 596	11 309
6. Financial services	−289	437	726
7.Computer and information services	3 279	6 512	3 233
8. Royalties and licensing fees	−10 636	429	11 065
9. Consulting services	5 206	18 623	13 417
10. Advertising and public opinion polling	358	2 313	1 955
11. Audio-visual and related services	−181	97	278
12.Other business services	5 916	24 688	18 772
13. Government services, n.i.e.	110	950	840
B. Income	**43 282**	**108 582**	**65 299**
1.Compensation of employees	7 158	9 209	2 052
2.Investment income	36 124	99 372	63 248
C. Current transfers	**33 748**	**42 645**	**8 897**
1.General government	−247	43	291
2.Other sectors	33 996	42 602	8 606
II. Capital and financial account	**144 828**	**746 439**	**601 611**
A. Capital account	**3 958**	**4 204**	**247**
B. Financial account	**140 871**	**742 235**	**601 364**
1. Direct investment	**34 294**	**114 198**	**79 904**
1.1 Abroad	−43 898	4 163	48 061
1.2 In China	78 193	110 036	31 843
2. Portfolio investment	**38 691**	**98 112**	**59 420**
2.1 Assets	9 888	66 919	57 032
2.1.1 Equity securities	−33 815	12 241	46 056
2.1.2 Debt securities	43 703	54 678	10 976
2.1.2.1 Bonds and notes	36 956	47 917	10 961
2.1.2.2 Money market instruments	6 747	6 761	14
2.2 Liabilities	28 804	31 192	2 389
2.2.1 Equity securities	28 161	28 850	689

(To be continued)

① China's balance of payments statement is compiled in accordance with the principles of the fifth edition of the *Balance of Payments Manual* of the International Monetary Fund, recording all economic transactions between residents of the Chinese mainland (excluding residents of Hong Kong SAR, Macau SAR, and Taiwan province) and non-residents based on the principle of a double-entry system.

(continued)

Item	Balance	Credit	Debit
2.2.2 Debt securities	643	2 343	1 700
2.2.2.1 Bonds and notes	643	2 342	1 699
2.2.2.2 Money market instruments	0	1	1
3. Other investment	**67 885**	**529 925**	**462 040**
3.1 Assets	9 365	117 394	108 029
3.1.1 Trade credits	−54 435	0	54 435
Long-term	−3 810	0	3 810
Short-term	−50 625	0	50 625
3.1.2 Loans	12 996	44 962	31 965
Long-term	−31 504	0	31 504
Short-term	44 500	44 962	461
3.1.3 Currency and deposits	5 171	26 739	21 568
3.1.4 Other assets	45 633	45 694	61
Long-term	0	0	0
Short-term	45 633	45 694	61
3.2 Liabilities	58 520	412 531	354 011
3.2.1 Trade credits	32 058	32 058	0
Long-term	2 244	2 244	0
Short-term	29 814	29 814	0
3.2.2 Loans	3 749	322 245	318 496
Long-term	−9 688	13 495	23 183
Short-term	13 437	308 749	295 313
3.2.3 Currency and deposits	11 575	45 622	34 047
3.2.4 Other liabilities	11 138	12 606	1 468
Long-term	11 029	11 029	0
Short-term	109	1 577	1 468
III. Reserve assets	**−398 422**	**0**	**398 422**
3.1 Monetary gold	−4 876	0	4 876
3.2 Special drawing rights	−11 092	0	11 092
3.3 Reserve position in the fund	−402	0	402
3.4 Foreign exchange	−382 051	0	382 051
3.5 Other claims	0	0	0
IV. Net errors and omissions	−43 548	0	43 548

(Ⅲ) Evaluation of the Balance of Payments

In 2009, due to the international financial crisis, China's balance of payments transactions generally slowed down. Balance of payments transactions totaled USD 4 trillion, a decrease of 12 percent year on year. The balance of payments accounted for 81.9 percent of GDP, 18.9 percentage points lower than that in 2008. The transaction volume of the main items dropped compared with that in 2008. Based on the balance of payments statistics, trade in goods totaled

USD 2 158.1 billion, a decrease of 14 percent; trade in services totaled USD 288.5 billion, down 6 percent; the inflow of inward direct investment was USD 110 billion, a decline of 32 percent; and the outflow of overseas direct investment dropped by 14 percent to USD 48.1 billion.

Chart 1-1

China's Scale of BOP Transactions and Its Ratio to GDP

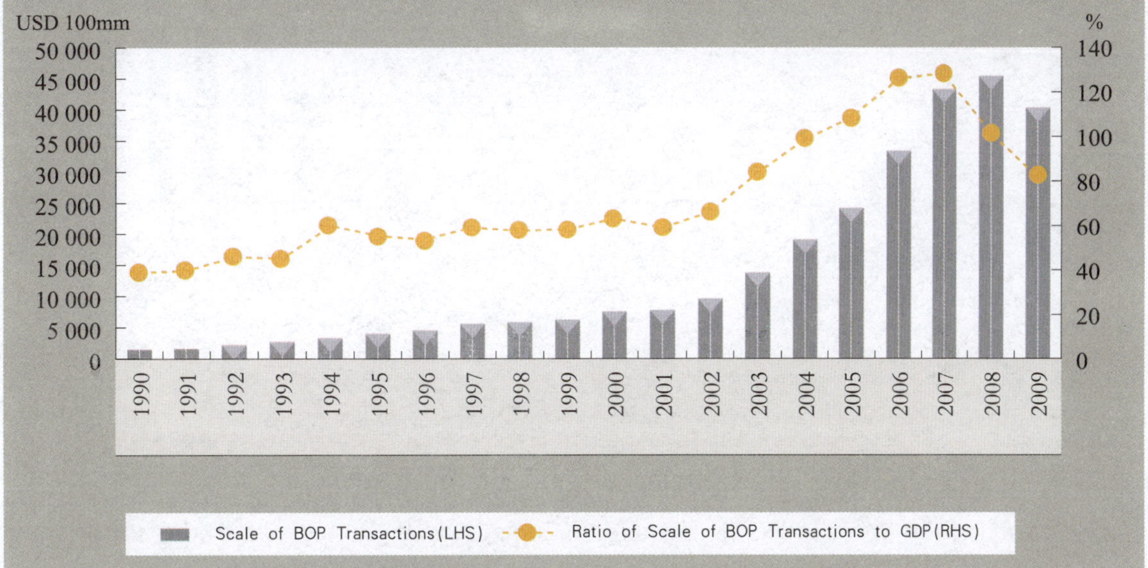

China's balance of payments transactions continued to post a "twin surplus" with a continued improvement. In 2009, the balance of payments surplus was recorded at USD 442 billion, a decrease of 3 percent year on year, whereas in 2008 it had increased 2 percent, and it accounted for 6.1 percent of GDP, down 3.5 percentage points from the previous year, continuing the decrease for the second consecutive year. Domestic demand contributed more than external demand to China's economic growth.

Table 1-2 Structure of the Surplus in the Balance of Payments from 2003 to 2009

Unit: USD 100 million

Item	2003	2004	2005	2006	2007	2008	2009
Overall surplus in the BOP	986	1 794	2 238	2 599	4 453	4 551	4 420
Balance in the current account	459	687	1 608	2 533	3 718	4 361	2 971
The ratio of current account balance to GDP	2.8%	3.6%	7.2%	9.5%	11.0%	9.6%	6.1%
Balance in the capital and financial account	527	1 107	630	67	735	190	1 448
The ratio of capital and financial account balance to GDP	3.2%	5.8%	2.8%	0.3%	2.2%	0.4%	3.0%

Chart 1–2

China's Current Account Balance and Its Ratio to GDP

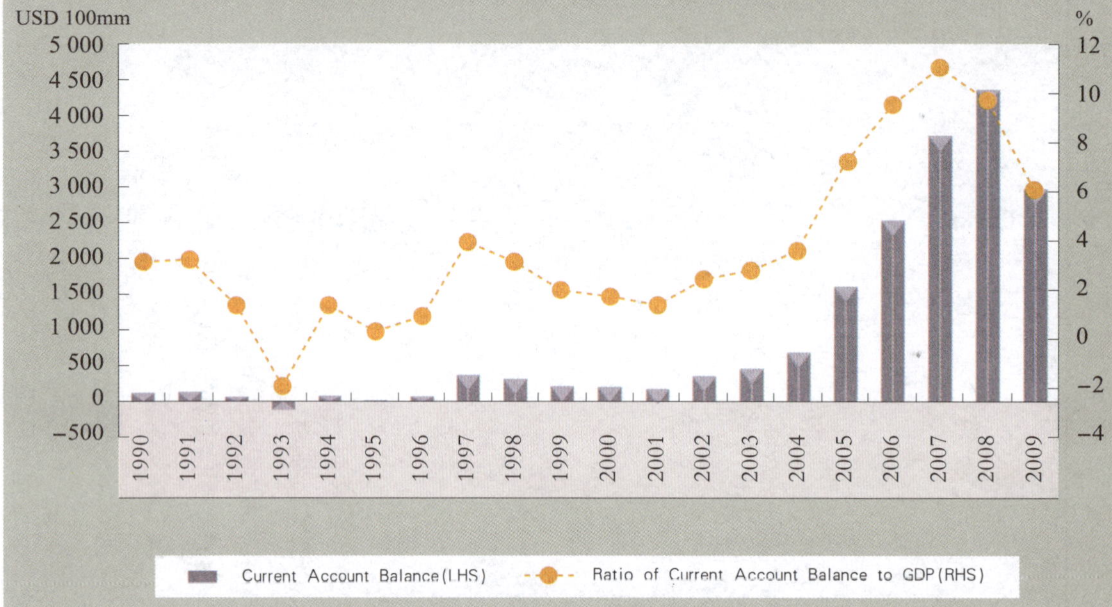

The performance of the balance of payments increasingly fluctuated due to the adjustments in the domestic and international macro environments. In the first half of 2009, due to the international financial crisis, the total of balance of payment transactions decreased 27 percent year on year, among which trade in goods and trade in services declined by 24 percent and 14 percent respectively, and the outstanding external debt by the end of June had decreased slightly by 4 percent from that at the end of 2008. In the second half of the year, owing to the upward momentum in domestic and international economic performance, the total scale of the balance of payments surpassed that in the first half of the year, recording a 6 percent increase year on year, among which trade in goods decreased 5 percent year on year, trade in services increased 2 percent year on year, and the outstanding of external debt increased 19 percent from that at the end of June.

Foreign capital net inflows recovered gradually, but imbalances in the balance of payments still posed a serious problem. Since the second quarter of 2009, foreign exchange net inflows had rebounded and the risk of a reverse in the balance payments has tended to be alleviated. In the first half of the year, the balance of payments surplus totaled USD 195.5 billion, a decrease of

26 percent year on year; in the second half of the year, the balance of payments surplus totaled USD 246.5 billion, an increase of 29 percent year on year. With respect to the main items, trade in goods, income, and current transfers in the second half of the year recorded higher surpluses than in the first half, and net inflows of inward foreign direct investment recorded an increase 1.7 times of that in the first half of the year. In general, the accumulated balance of payments surplus totaled more than USD 400 billion, marking a historical high.

Box Ⅲ

Characteristics of China's Abnormal Cross-Border Capital Flows

At present, due to the rapid development of global internationalization and financial freedom with enriched financial products and facilitated financial transactions, global asset allocations and investment have become popular. Cross-border capital flows increased by many times with the enhanced openness of the Chinese economy. According to the statistics of the SAFE's balance of payments reporting system, in 2009, China's cross-border revenue and payments totaled 32 million transactions, amounting to USD 3.6 trillion. It is inevitable that some abnormal cross-border capital may flow in with the normal trade and investment. Meanwhile, with the Chinese economy more market-oriented, market entities, such as banks, enterprises, and individuals, became more sensitive to price signals and there was an increase in transactions driven by risk aversion or profit arbitrage. In recent years, the Chinese economy performed prominently throughout the world, and there was an expectation that there would be a revaluation of the RMB exchange rate and the interest rate spread between domestic and international markets, which together provided room for arbitrage and inevitable abnormal cross-border capital flows.

Abnormal cross-border capital flows are different from "hot money" in some emerging markets. First, they flow via legal channels. Since China maintains controls over cross-border capital and financial transactions, abnormal cross-border capital usually flows via the current account, direct investment, bank operations, and personal transactions, which are usually deregulated, instead of via short-term capital account items such as portfolio investment and external debt. Second, most of it is long-term investment. Against the background of the rapid development of the Chinese economy, in the long run there will always be room for RMB exchange rate and interest rate arbitrage, and abnormal cross-border capital will focus on long-term profits instead of frequent flows. Third, the major operators of the arbitrage capital are domestic institutions. For instance, domestic commercial banks withdraw their foreign assets to extend domestic foreign exchange loans to receive higher interest income; foreign capital flows via the international lists of domestic institutions or from financing from the SPV establishment. Fourth, capital inflows support enterprises development. Since China's investment and financing mechanisms are still under-developed, it is difficult for many enterprises, small and medium private enterprises in particular, to access financing, thus some financing demands need to be met by private financing (including foreign financing) beyond the official mechanisms, which, to some extent, compensates for the shortage in domestic investment and financing mechanisms. However, regulation and guidance are still required.

In general, there should be closer monitoring and analysis of abnormal cross-border capital flows. The government should launch well-targeted measures to achieve better guidance and to seek both temporary and permanent solutions through cooperative administration by the SAFE, the Ministry of Commerce, the General Administration of Customs, the SAIC, and financial regulatory authorities so as to improve monitoring and control capabilities.

Ⅱ. Analysis of the Major Items in the Balance of Payments

(I) Trade in Goods

In 2009, the overall China's trades showed a trend of a general decline. Based on the balance of payments statistics, exports and imports of goods totaled USD 2 158.1 billion, a decrease of 14 percent year on year. In particular, exports totaled USD 1 203.8 billion, a decrease of 16 percent, and imports totaled USD 954.3 billion, a decline of 11 percent, representing a surplus of USD 249.5 billion, which was a 31 percent decrease year on year. According to the statistics of the General Administration of Customs, China's trade in goods showed the following characteristics in 2009:

Trade in goods saw a significant decline in the surplus because imports decreased less than exports. In 2009, exports and imports of goods amounted to USD 2 207.2 billion, a 14 percent year–on–year decrease, among which exports and imports totaled USD 1 201.7 billion and USD 1 005.6 billion respectively, dropping by 11 percent and 16 percent. Imports declined 5 percentage points less than exports. The trade in goods surplus totaled USD 196.1 billion for the entire year, a decrease of 34 percent USD 102 billion less than the decrease in the last year. Since March 2009, trade in goods stabilized after the decline since October 2008, but it has not fully recovered to the pre–crisis level.

Chart 2–1

China's Import and Export since the Reform and Opening-up

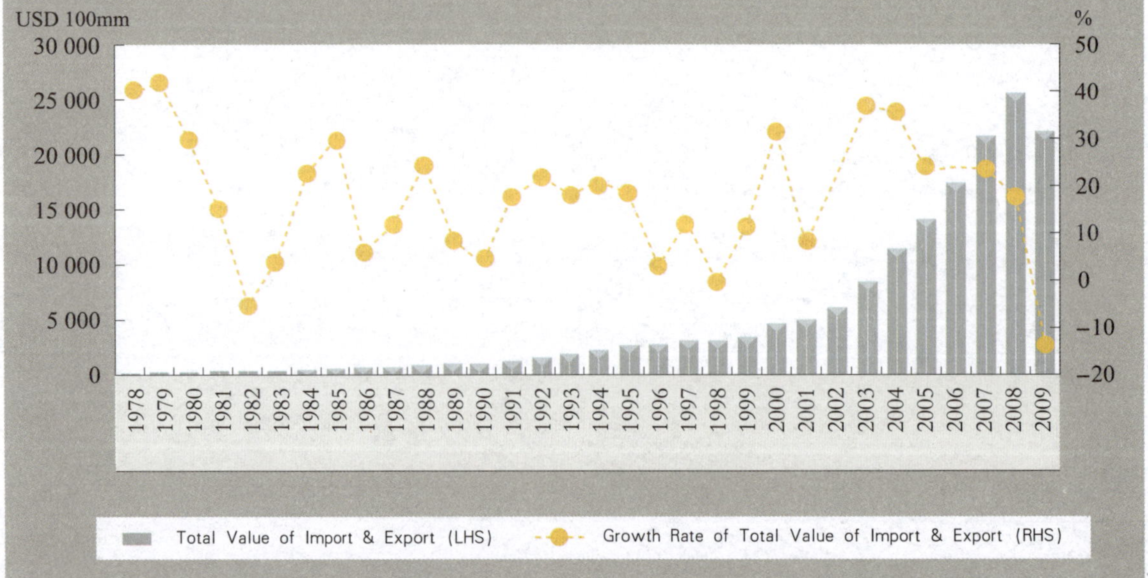

Ordinary trade recorded a deficit and processing trade recorded less of a surplus. In 2009, exports and imports of ordinary goods totaled USD 1 063.7 billion, a decrease of 14 percent. Exports of ordinary goods totaled USD 529.8 billion, dropping by 20 percent and decreasing more than total exports. Imports totaled USD 533.9 billion, decreasing by 7 percent and decreasing more than total imports. Exports declined more than imports by 13 percentage points, and ordinary trade recorded a deficit of USD 4.1 billion instead of the surplus of USD 89.9 billion in 2008. China's processing trade exports and imports totaled USD 909.3 billion, down 14 percent. In particular, exports totaled USD 587 billion, a decrease of 13 percent; imports totaled USD 322.3 billion, a decrease of 15 percent. Processing trade registered a surplus of USD 264.7 billion, a year-on-year decline of 11 percent.

Foreign-funded enterprises recorded a smaller decline in the surplus, the deficit of state-owned enterprises grew, and imports by private enterprises increased. In 2009, foreign-funded enterprises maintained the same level of adjustment for exports and imports as in the overall situation: exports totaled USD 672.2 billion, a decrease of 15 percent; imports totaled USD 545.2 billion, a decrease of 12 percent; the surplus amounted to USD 127 billion, a drop of 26 percent, which was 8 percentage points lower than the decline in the total surplus. State-owned enterprises were more seriously affected by the international financial crisis: exports amounted to USD 191 billion, a decrease of 26 percent, which was 10 percentage points higher than the overall decrease in exports; imports amounted to USD 288.5 billion, a decrease of 19 percent and 8 percentage points higher than that for overall imports; the surplus was USD 97.5 billion, a net increase of USD 0.9 billion. Exports by private enterprises exports totaled USD 338.4 billion, a decrease of 12 percent and imports by private enterprises amounted to USD 171.9 billion, an increase of 8 percent, resulting in a surplus of USD 166.5 billion, which was a USD 54.9 billion year-on-year decrease.

Imports from European and American markets declined slightly, and trade with neighboring countries and regions recorded a deficit. In 2009 the European Union remained China's top trading partner, with bilateral trade totaling USD 364 billion, down 15 percent, among which bilateral imports declined by only 3.7 percent and China posted a surplus of USD 108.5 billion, down 32 percent. Sino-U.S. trade totaled USD 298.3 billion, down 11 percent and ranking as China's second largest trading partner. In particular, imports declined by only 4.8 percent and China posted a surplus of USD 143.4 billion, down 16 percent. Among its top ten bilateral trade partners, China posted deficits with Japan, ASEAN, Korea, Taiwan of China, Australia, and Brazil.

Imports of primary products continued to grow, exports of labor–intensive products fell at lower rate, and the terms of trade again deteriorated. In 2009, imports of primary products basically continued to grow: imports of iron ore totaled 0.6 billion tons, with a growth rate of 42 percent; crude oil totaled 0.2 billion tons, with a growth rate of 14 percent; coal totaled 0.13 billion tons, with a growth rate of 210 percent; copper totaled 4.29 million tons, with a growth rate of 63 percent; grain totaled 2.07 million tons, with a growth rate of 27 percent. Imports of machinery and electronic products and high–tech products totaled USD 491.4 billion and USD 309.8 billion respectively, a 9 percent year–on–year decrease for each. Labor–intensive exports declined less than overall exports: garment exports totaled USD 107.1 billion, with the rate of the decrease at 11 percent; textile exports totaled USD 60 billion, with the rate of the decrease at 8 percent; shoes exports totaled USD 28 billion, with the rate the decrease at 6 percent; machinery and electronic products and high–tech products totaled USD 713.1 billion and USD 376.9 billion, with the rate of the decrease at 13 percent and 9 percent respectively. Although China's terms of trade improved by 8.7 percent year on year, the structure and pricing mechanisms basically did not improve, and the price of international staple goods gradually increased, which led to a deterioration in the terms of trade after the short–term improvement between the end of 2008 and the beginning of 2009. In December 2009, China's terms of trade index had declined by 14 percent than February.

(II) Trade in Services

In 2009, China's receipts from trade in services totaled USD 129.5 billion, a decrease of 12 percent year on year; payments for trade in services were almost the same as in 2008, totaling USD 158.9 billion; the item posted a deficit of USD 29.4 billion, an increase of 149 percent. China's trade in services was characterized by the following:

Trade in services decreased less than trade in goods and the structure of foreign trade improved. In 2009, the scale of trade in services totaled USD 288.5 billion, down 6 percent, and 8 percentage points lower than that of trade in goods. Although receipts and payments for trade in services generally decreased, some items showed an upward trend. In 2009, payments for construction, finance, and travel continued to increase, with growth rates of over 20 percent; receipts from government services, financial services, and insurance services also increased, with growth rates over 15 percent.

The rapid growth in the deficit of trade in services shows that China's trade in services still lacks a general comparative advantage. The deficit of trade in services increased by 1.49 times year on year, coming from transportation, royalties and licensing fees, insurance services, and travel, with the deficits posting USD 23 billion, USD 10.6 billion, USD 9.7 billion, and USD 4 billion respectively. In particular, travel posted a deficit for the first time since 1982. Receipts from travel totaled USD 39.7 billion, a decrease of 3 percent and payments for travel totaled USD 43.7 billion, an increase of 21 percent, recording a deficit of USD 4 billion, whereas there had been a surplus of USD 4.7 billion in the first half of the year. In 2009, affected by the global recession, inbound visitors decreased significantly. With the improvements in income standards and the structure of residents' consumption, payments became diversified instead of being concentrated in trade in goods, and trade in services accounted for an increasing proportion because of the growth in payments for the purpose of private travel. In 2009, China's outbound travel visitors grew by 4 percent. Grouped by receipts and payments from specific countries, China posted large deficits with the United States, Macau SAR, and Australia.

Chart 2-2

China's Receipts and Payments of Travel Item from Main Countries/Regions

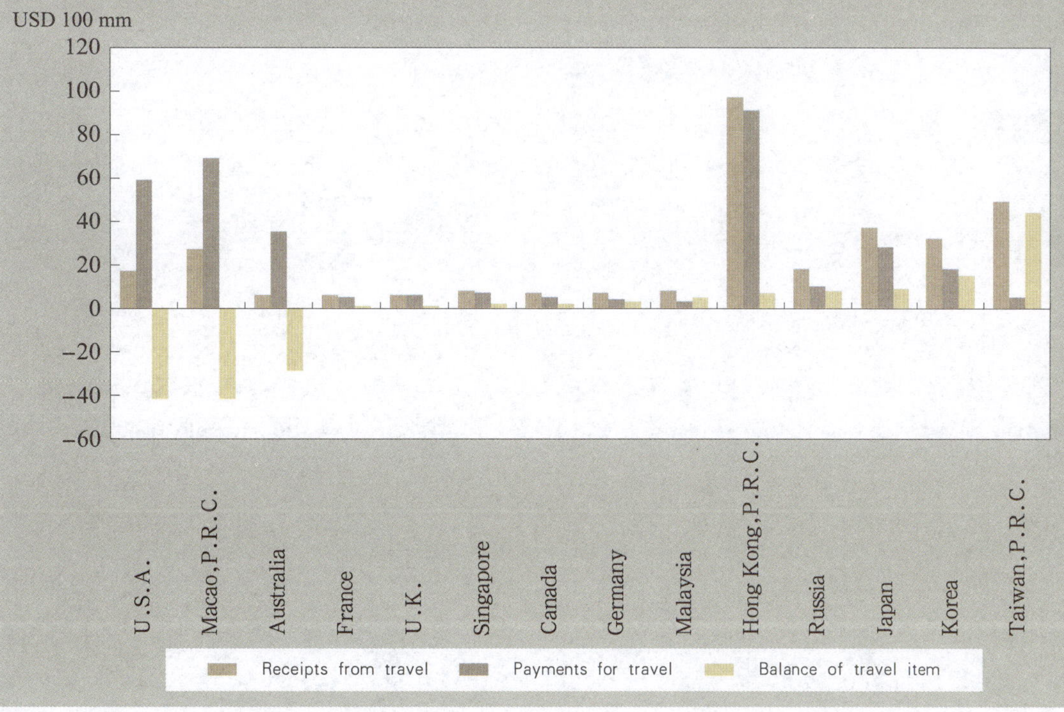

Deficit items decreased. In 2009, among all 13 items of trade in services, 6 recorded a surplus, with other business services, consulting services, construction services, and computer and information services posting surpluses of USD 5.9 billion, USD 5.2 billion, USD 3.6 billion, and USD 3.3 billion respectively. In 2008, 8 items recorded a surplus, among which travel, audio-visual and related services, and communication services became deficit in 2009.

Transportation and travel were the major items in trade in services, by a slightly decreasing proportion. In 2009 receipts from transportation and travel accounted for 18 and 31 percent of the total receipts from trade in services respectively, and their payments accounted for 29 and 27 percent respectively. The two items accounted for 53 percent of the total trade in services, one percentage point lower than that in the previous year. At the same time, the proportion of construction services, royalties and licensing fees, and computer and information services increased slightly.

China's trade in services with major countries/regions remained basically stable and highly concentrated. The volume of trade in services with China's top 10 partners accounted for 78 percent of the total volume of trade in services, among which the top 5 partners in terms of receipts were Hong Kong SAR of China, the United States, Japan, Singapore, and Korea, and the top 5 partners in terms of payments for trade in services were still Hong Kong SAR of China, the United States, Japan, Korea, and Macao SAR of China.

Box Ⅳ

The Characteristics and Evolution of China's Individual Foreign Exchange Business

In recent years, the scale of China's individual receipts and payments of foreign exchange (individual cross-border payments and receipts) and the scale of sales and purchase of foreign exchange (transfers of domestic and foreign currency by individuals) continued to grow. In order to support and facilitate domestic individuals legally holding and using foreign exchange and to enhance administration of individual foreign exchange businesses and services, the SAFE continued to improve individual foreign exchange policies. At present, every person is allowed to purchase or sell foreign exchange amounting to USD 50 000 per year. Within the annual quota, a person deal directly with the banks on the basis of his/her own effective identification certificate, and this quota almost satisfies the individual demand for foreign exchange.

Currently, China's individual receipts and payments as well as purchases and sales of foreign exchange are characterized by the following: First, many participants are involved in the business, including not only domestic citizens but also foreign visitors. Second, different business categories are involved because individual cross-border receipts and payments as well as purchases and sales of foreign exchange may be current account or capital and financial account transactions. Third, not only the international and domestic economic and financial situations as well as the exchange rate fluctuation affect individual foreign exchange business, but also seasonal factors influence it.

The scale of individual foreign exchange busines sgenerally tends to increase with the relatively rapid growth of individual payments.① From 2006 to 2009, the total volume of individual receipts and payments of foreign exchange grew by 11 percent annually, among which individual receipts of foreign exchangeincreased by 3 percent annually and payments increased by 45 percent annually. In recent years, with the increase in foreign study and tourism, individual paymentsin foreign exchange have continued to grow. Against this background, individual foreign exchange business posted a surplus, at a decreasing annual rate of 13 percent from 2006 to 2009, and in 2009 in particular, individual receipts of foreign exchangerecorded a surplus of USD 40.2 billion, a drop of 41 percent year on year.

Individual purchases and sales of foreign exchange shared the same features as individual receipts and payments, with significantly increased individual purchases of foreign exchange.② The scale of individual foreign exchange purchases and sales increased 21 percent annually during 2006–2009, among which individual sales increased by 8 percent annually and individual purchases increased by 79 percent annually. In 2009, individual sales and purchases of foreign exchange decreased 20 percent and 45 percent respectively, posting a surplus of USD 40.7 billion, down 53 percent year on year.

① Data source: ITRS (International Transaction Reporting System).

② Data source: Foreign Exchange Sale and Purchase Statistical System.

Chart 2–3

Individual Receipts and Payments of FX, 2006-2009

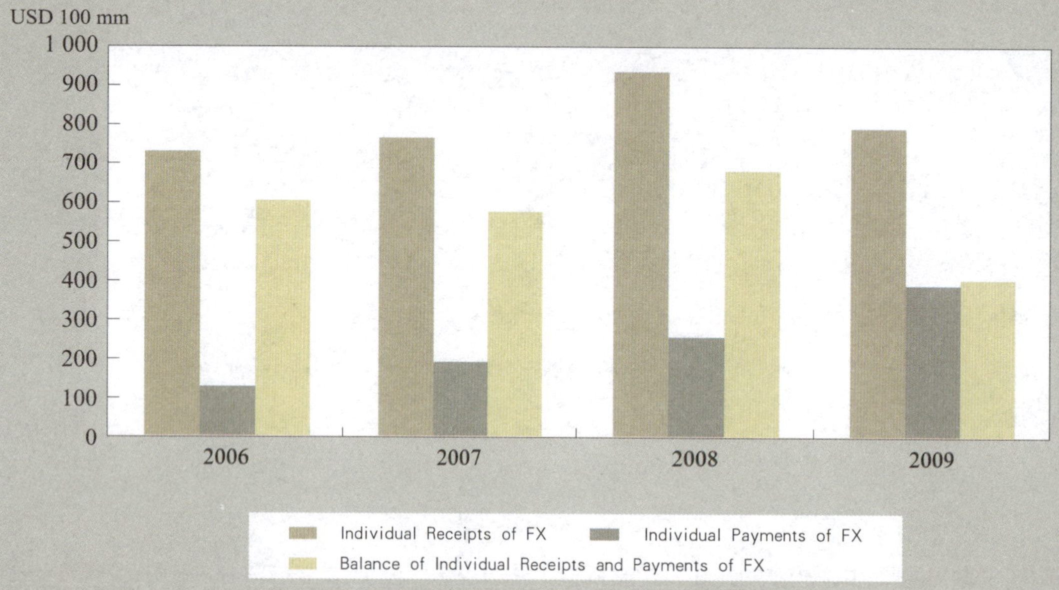

Chart 2–4

Individual Purchases and Sales of FX, 2006-2009

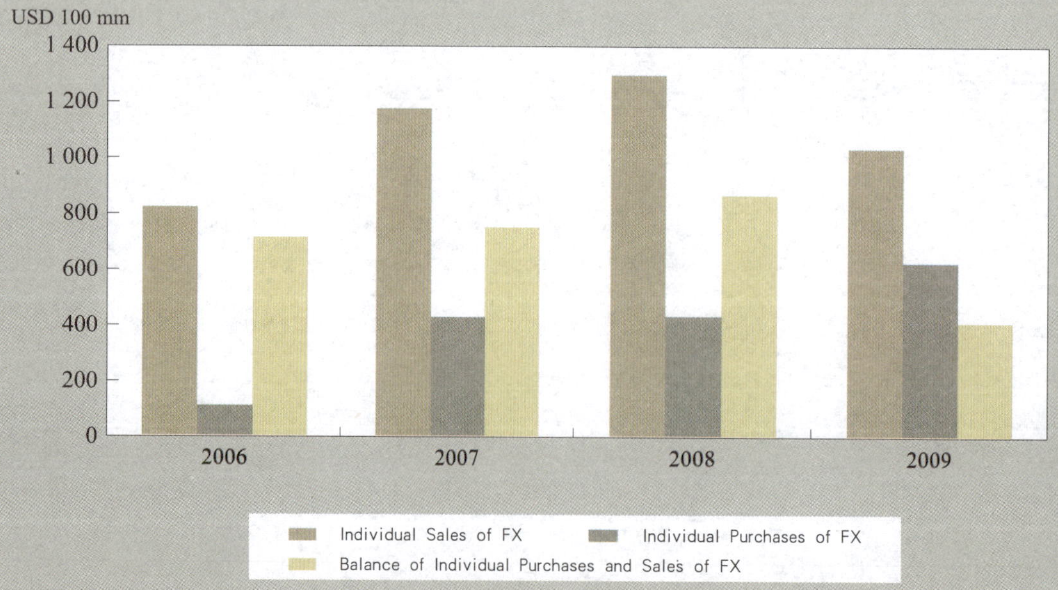

(Ⅲ) Direct Investment

1. Inward foreign direct investment declined

Based on the balance of payments statistics, in 2009, the inflow of inward foreign direct investment totaled USD 110 billion, a decrease of 32 percent year on year; the withdrawal and liquidation of equity capital under inward foreign direct investment was USD 31.8 billion, a rise of 143 percent year on year, up 126 percentage points from the growth in the previous year; net inflows totaled USD 78.2 billion, down 47 percent.① Inward foreign direct investment in 2009 was characterized by the following:

Inward foreign direct investment in both the financial sector and the non-financial sector declined. The inflow in the financial sector amounted to USD 4.1 billion, a decrease of 72 percent; the inflow in the non-financial sector totaled USD 105.9 billion, a decrease of 28 percent.

Chart 2-5

China's Foreign Direct Investment Inflows

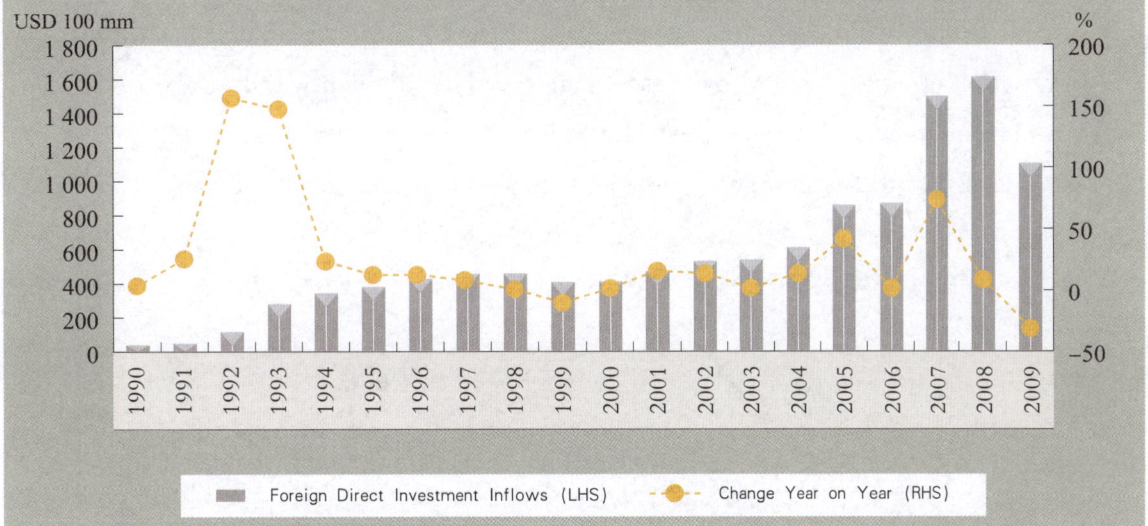

① According to the statistical coverage of the balance of payments, inflows under foreign direct investment in China (credits) refer to investments that include including equity capital, reinvested earnings, and other capital related to establishing foreign-funded enterprises in China; outflows (debits) include the withdrawal and liquidation of equity capital. Currently, due to the influence of statistical points, statistical coverage, statistical quality, and so forth, there are certain differences between the data on inward foreign direct investment based on the balance of payments statistics and the data on the actual utilization of foreign capital disseminated by the Ministry of Commerce.

The sources of the non-financial foreign direct investment were relatively concentrated. In 2009, the top 10 countries/regions as sources of inward foreign direct investment were, in order, Hong Kong SAR, the United States, Singapore, Japan, Taiwan of China, the British Virgin Islands, Korea, Germany, France, and the United Kingdom, accounting for 91 percent of the total inflow of inward foreign direct investment.

The industrial distribution displayed various characteristics. Foreign investors focused on management of water conservancy, the environment, and public facilities, financing, leasing, and business services, and construction, agriculture, forestry, animal husbandry, and the fishery industries, with growth rates of 123 percent, 49 percent, 19 percent, 12 percent, and 11 percent respectively. Real foreign capital utilization in household services and other services, mining, manufacturing, and real estate dropped significantly, dropping by 54 percent, 54 percent, 31 percent, and 30 percent respectively.

The withdrawal and liquidation of equity capital and shareholder loans under inward foreign direct investment recorded a large net outflow. Because some foreign banks such as Bank of America withdrew their equity holdings of domestic banks totaling USD 10.4 billion (33 percent of the outflow of foreign capital direct investment), the outflow of withdrawals and liquidation of equity capital increased sharply. Without such withdrawals, inward FDI withdrawals and liquidation totaled USD 21.2 billion, an increase at the rate of 62 percent, and the main source was the outflow of shareholder loans in the non-financial sectors.

2. Overseas direct investment decreased

In 2009, China's overseas direct investment totaled USD 48.1 billion, a decrease of 14 percent year on year, and remittances for the withdrawal and liquidation of overseas direct investment amounted to USD 4.2 billion, a rise of 91 percent, resulting in a net outflow of USD 43.9 billion and a decrease of 18 percent year on year. China's overseas direct investment was characterized by the following:

Investment from the financial sector and the non-financial sector displayed different characteristics. Overseas direct investment by the financial sector totaled USD 4.7 billion, a decrease at the rate of 69 percent, whereas overseas direct investment by the non-financial sector amounted to USD 43.4 billion, at a growth rate of 7 percent.

In terms of investment destinations, China's overseas direct investment by the financial sector was concentrated in regions with developed financial markets, such as Hong Kong SAR, the United Kingdom, and the United States. Overseas direct investment by the non-financial sector focused on Asia and Latin America. Investment in Asia, Latin America, and other regions accounted for 59 percent, 25 percent, and 16 percent respectively.

In terms of the industrial distribution, the overseas direct investment by China's non-financial sector was diversified in many industries, including the commercial services industry (aimed at holding investment), mining, wholesale and retail trade, manufacturing, transportation, and real estate. In particular, the commercial services industry and mining were the main industries, which accounted for 55 percent and 25 percent respectively.

In terms of investment, in 2009 China's non-financial sector made overseas direct investments mainly by acquisitions, which accounted for 40 percent.

(Ⅳ) Portfolio Investment

In 2009, China recorded a net inflow of USD 38.7 billion, a drop of 9 percent year on year. In particular, the net inflow under China's outward portfolio investment was USD 9.9 billion, down 70 percent; and the net inflow under inward portfolio investment was USD 28.8 billion, increasing by 191 percent.

1. Outward equity security investment increased sharply and debt security investment recorded a net inflow

Outward equity security investment and debt security investment flowed in and out markedly. In particular, outward equity security investment recorded a net outflow of USD 33.8 billion, whereas it recorded a net outflow of USD 1.1 billion in the previous year; outward debt security investment posted a net inflow of USD 43.7 billion, up 29 percent. The main reason can be attributed to the adjustments in the allocation of foreign assets by different domestic sectors. On the one hand, with the rapid development of outward equity investment and a more active attitude, domestic non-banking sectors were becoming major investors in terms of outward equity security investment. On the other hand, domestic commercial banks remained major investors in outward debt security investment. Because there were still risks in the international financial market and demand for foreign exchange loans by domestic enterprises became stronger, commercial banks decreased their outstanding outward debt security assets. In 2009, outstanding domestic foreign exchange loans increased by USD 104.5 billion whereas foreign exchange deposits only increased by USD 16.2 billion.

2. Net inflows under inward portfolio investment increased

In 2009, the net inflow under inward portfolio investment totaled USD 28.8 billion. In particular, the net inflow of equity security investment was USD 28.2 billion and the net inflow of debt security investment was USD 0.6 billion. The main source for the net inflow of equity security investment was funds raised by overseas listings by Chinese enterprises and some of the purchases of the foreign-listed shares of the China Construction Bank by foreign institutions from the Bank of America.① In addition, inward investment by QFIIs increased as well, posting a net inflow of USD 3.3 billion. Debt security investments recorded a decrease in net inflows by 46 percent, mainly due to the more rapid growth in repayment of principal rather than new borrowing.

Box V

The Influence of Adjustments in the Banking Sector on the Allocation of Foreign Exchange Assets

In 2009, China posted a surplus of USD 144.8 billion under the capital and financial account, increasing by 6.6 times year on year, among which portfolio investment recorded a surplus of USD 38.7 billion and other investment recorded a surplus of USD 67.9 billion. The significant surge in the surplus of the capital and financial account was due to the fact that the banking sector transferred its foreign assets, including overseas portfolio investment and interbank lending, to domestic assets.

① According to the statistical principle of the BPM5, an investment should be regarded as direct investment by nonresidents to residents when nonresidents hold over 10 percent of the share of the resident institutions with voting rights. That with less than 10 percent is regarded as portfolio investment. Based on this principle, Bank of America divestment from the China Construction Bank and other nonresident investments thereafter should be recorded as a decrease in inward direct investment on the one hand and an increase in inward portfolio investment by nonresidents on the other.

Due to the international financial crisis, foreign assets in the banking sector faced increasing risks and decreasing revenue. With the United States implementing a quantitative easing monetary policy, the one-year LIBOR decreased from 1.9 percent at the beginning of 2009 to 1 percent in December 2009, and the weighted average interest rate for domestic one-year USD loans declined from 3 percent at the beginning of 2009 to 1.9 in December, 1 percentage point higher than the overseas interbank lending rate.

Based on the above, China's banking sector reduced its foreign assets by USD 66.3 billion, among which the overseas medium- (long-) term debt security position decreased by USD 44.2 billion, overseas loans (mainly interbank lending) decreased by USD 12.9 billion, and overseas currency and deposits decreased by USD 9.2 billion, which accounted for 67 percent, 19 percent, and 14 percent respectively. Meanwhile the external liabilities of overseas portfolio investment and other investment of the banking sector increased by USD 12.1 billion. In general, the banking sector recorded a net inflow of USD 78.4 billion, accounting for 74 percent of the surplus in portfolio investment and other investment and 54 percent of the surplus under the capital and financial account.

Funds transferred from abroad became the major source of domestic foreign exchange loans. In 2009, outstanding domestic foreign exchange loans increased by USD 104.5 billion, among which funds transferred from abroad contributed over 70 percent of the growth. On the one hand, the banking sector transferred large scale funds to facilitate import payments or overseas investments by extending foreign exchange loans to enterprises, substituting foreign exchange purchases and putting pressures on net foreign exchange purchases. From the second quarter of 2009, the banks' surplus from the purchase and sale for clients again surpassed the surplus of receipts and payments, which was different from the situation since July 2008. Analyzed by sales and purchases respectively, the volume of foreign exchange sales gradually recovered season by season, with a stable ratio (foreign exchange sales on behalf of customer/cross-border foreign exchange receipts), whereas the volume of foreign exchange purchases increased slowly, with a decreased purchase rate (foreign exchange purchases on behalf of customer/cross-border foreign exchange payments). On the other hand, the ratio of foreign exchange loans to deposits in the banking sector as well as the risks of a mismatch of foreign exchange assets and liabilities were increased by transferring funds from abroad. Once the interest rate and exchange rate of the USD pick up growth and the demand for domestic foreign exchange loans declines, the banking sector will need to reallocate its foreign exchange assets, leading to foreign exchange outflows and a decrease in the balance of payment surplus.

(V) External Debt

At the end of 2009, China's outstanding external debt totaled USD 428.6 billion, among which the outstanding registered external debt posted USD 266.9 billion with an increasing rate of 2 percent year on year, and trade credit was USD 161.7 billion,① up 25 percent.

By maturity, the outstanding medium– and long–term (residual maturity) external debt totaled USD 169.4 billion, accounting for 40 percent of the total outstanding; the outstanding short–term external debt totaled USD 259.3 billion, accounting for 60 percent of the total outstanding.

Chart 2–6

China's Outstanding External Debt and Short-term (Residual Maturity) Debt Ratio

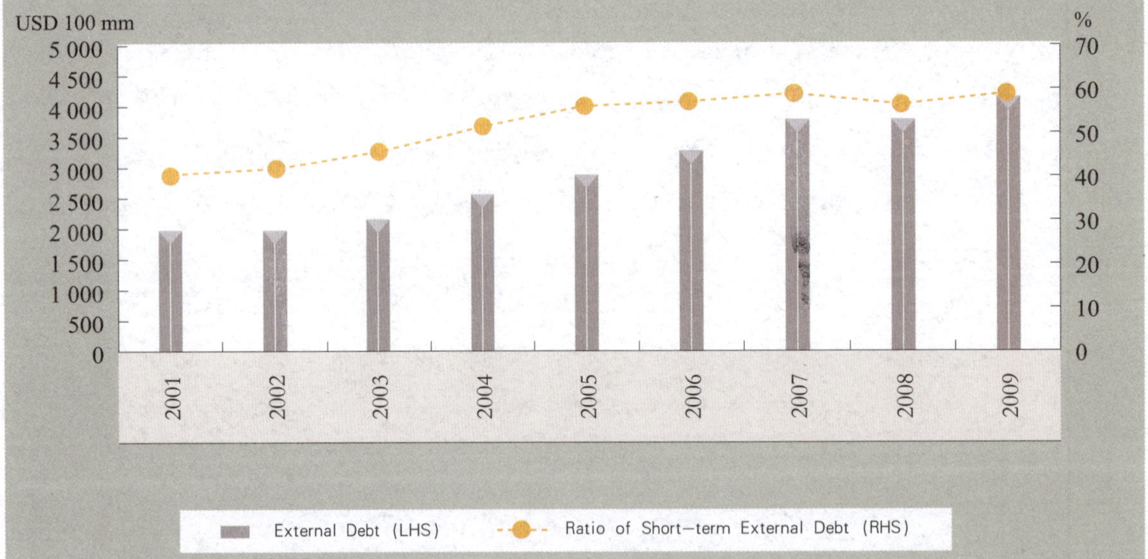

In terms of debt instruments, the main type was international commercial loans. As of the end of

① In 2009, the SAFE adjusted its methodology for the sample survey of trade credit. According to the new methodology, outstanding trade credit totaled USD 161.7 billion. To insure comparability of the data, outstanding trade credit at the end of 2008 was updated to USD 129.6 billion instead of USD 114.1 billion.

2009, outstanding international commercial loans totaled USD 198.6 billion, accounting for 74 percent of the registered external debt, 3 percentage points less than that in the previous year.

Chart 2-7

Components of Registered External Debt by Type of Debt in China

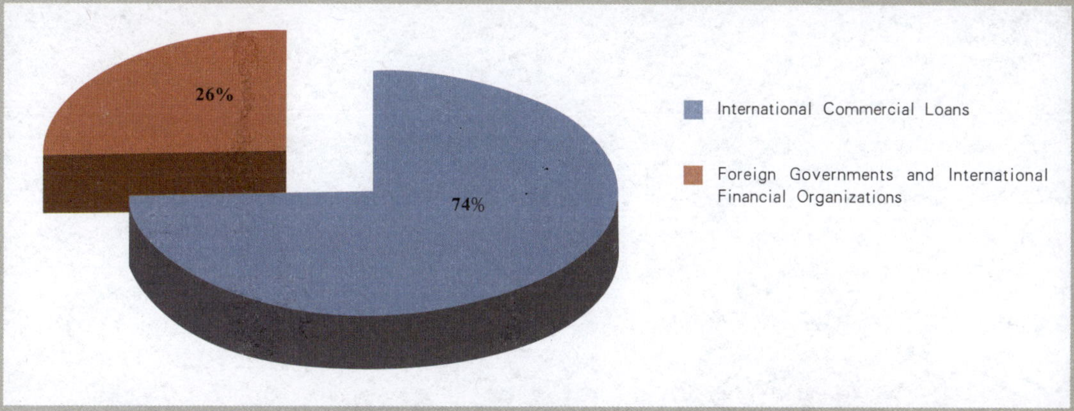

In terms of debtors, Chinese-funded financial institutions and foreign-funded enterprises were the major debtors. As of the end of 2009, the outstanding external debt of Chinese-funded financial institutions and foreign-funded enterprises posted USD 94.1 billion and USD 93.2 billion respectively, both accounting for 35 percent.

Chart 2-8

Components of Registered External Debt by Type of Debtor in China

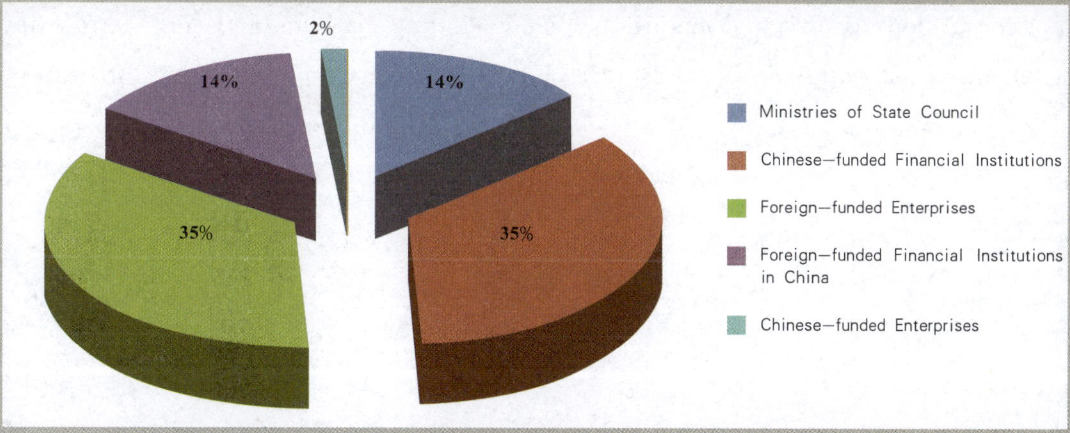

In terms of currency composition, the major part was external debt denominated in USD . As of the end of 2009, external debt denominated in USD accounted for 68 percent of the total registered external debt, down 0.5 percentage point from the end of 2008. External debt denominated in Yen accounted for 12 percent, ranking the second and 0.1 percentage point lower than that in 2008.

Chart 2-9

Components of Registered External Debt by Currency in China

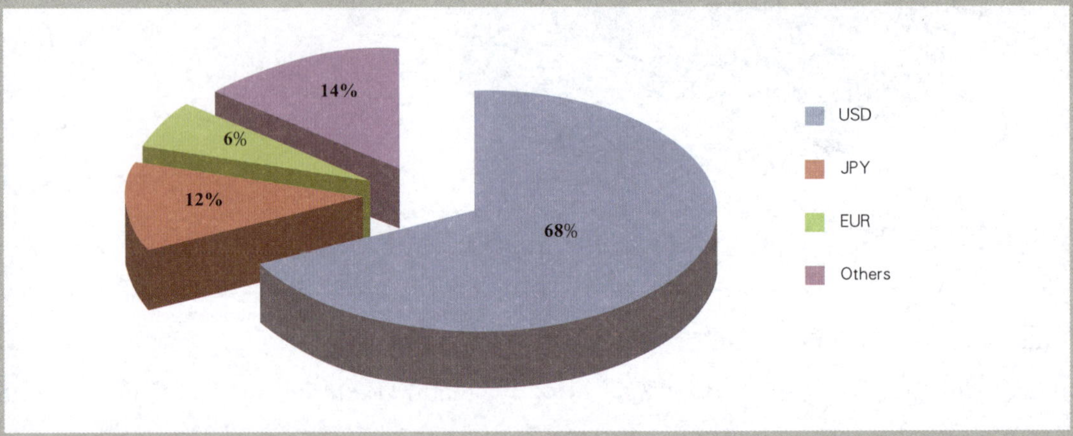

Medium-and-long-term external debts were mainly invested in infrastructure construction, including traffic and transportation and storage and postal services. Based on the classification of national industries, of the USD 188.1 billion of outstanding registered medium-and-long-term external debt (contractual maturity), the outstanding medium-and-long-term external debt borrowed for manufacturing was USD 39.1 billion, or 21 percent; that for traffic and transportation and storage and postal services was USD 23.8 billion, or 13 percent.

Chart 2–10

Components of Medium- and- long- term External Debts (Contractual Maturity) by Industry Structure in China

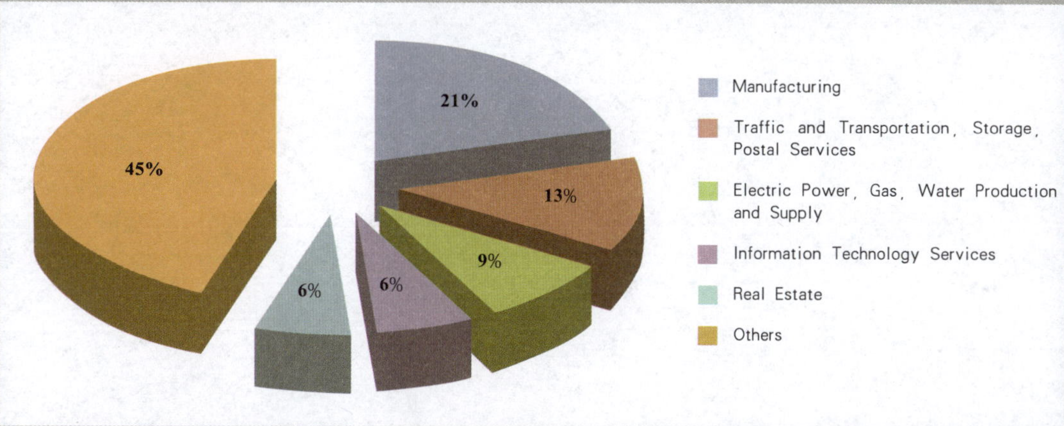

In 2009, China's external debt exhibited the following features:

The scale of gross external debt resumed an upward trend following its downward trend. The outstanding external debt continued to decrease in the first quarter of 2009, following the downward trend since the fourth quarter of 2008, whereas in the second and third quarters the outstanding increased slightly compared with that at the end of 2008, and it increased significantly in the fourth quarter. The growth rate of the outstanding external debt increased by −1.1 percent, 5.6 percent, −0.6 percent, and 5.9 percent respectively in the four quarters of 2009. In particular, outstanding trade credit increased by 2.7 percent, 17.5 percent, −3.6 percent, and 7.3 percent quarter by quarter, and the outstanding of Chinese–funded financial institutions grew by −5.0 percent, 5.5 percent, 4.8 percent, and 8.1 percent quarter by quarter.

The main drivers for the growth in external debt were trade credit and the external debt of Chinese–funded financial institutions. Calculated by their comparative coverage, by the end of 2009, China's outstanding external debt had increased by USD 38.5 billion, among which outstanding trade credit increased by USD 32.1 billion, accounting for 83 percent of the total increase and the outstanding external debt of Chinese–funded financial institutions increased by USD 11.3 billion, accounting for 29 percent of the total increase, which together accounted for 112 percent of the total increase.

Ⅲ. Operations of the Foreign Exchange Market and the RMB Exchange Rate

(I) Reform and Development of the Inter-bank Foreign Exchange Market

1. Participants in the foreign exchange market were increased and diversified

At the end of 2009, the number of participants on the spot, forward, foreign exchange swap, and currency swap inter-bank foreign exchange market reached 276, 73, 71, and 20 respectively. Apart from the number of participants on the currency swap market equaling that of the last year, the participants on the three other markets increased by 8, 4, and 2 respectively. The number of non-financial institution participants such as financial corporations for enterprise groups continued to grow, with an increase of 7 in 2009.

2. A new version of the foreign exchange trading system was put online and the operational efficiency of the foreign exchange market was further improved

On April 27, 2009, the third edition of a new foreign exchange trading system was formally implemented, with an updated utility and user interface system and a newly introduced strategy for order trading, which diversified the features of the trading system and made operations more user friendly. After it was put online, the new system maintained stable operations and improved trading efficiency as well as receiving a positive reaction from the market.

3. Net settlement of OTC transactions was implemented and the operational costs and risks of the foreign exchange market were reduced

On June 1, 2009, net settlement of OTC transactions on the spot foreign exchange market was formally launched. A counterparty settlement arrangement on the basis of multilateral net settlements was conducive to reducing credit risks and settlement risks of foreign exchange transactions, strengthening the guarding against systematic risks, and further promoting development for the foreign exchange market and especially for the derivative market.

4. The platform of the foreign exchange market was enriched and equal competition was improved

Three monetary brokerage companies were approved to conduct foreign exchange brokerage business, which further improved the liquidity and efficiency of the foreign exchange market.

Meanwhile, the fees that the China Foreign Exchange Trading Center (CFETC) charges for labor costs of derivative products in the inter–bank foreign exchange market were standardized, which helped to build up a fair and orderly market environment that is interactive and complementary between the CFETC and the monetary brokerage companies.

(Ⅱ) Trends in the RMB Exchange Rate against the Major Foreign Currencies

1. The RMB exchange rate against the USD remained basically steady

At the end of 2009, the RMB central parity against the USD closed at 6.8282, an appreciation of 64 bps from 6.8346 at the end of 2008.

Chart 3–1

Trends in the RMB/USD Central Parity in 2009

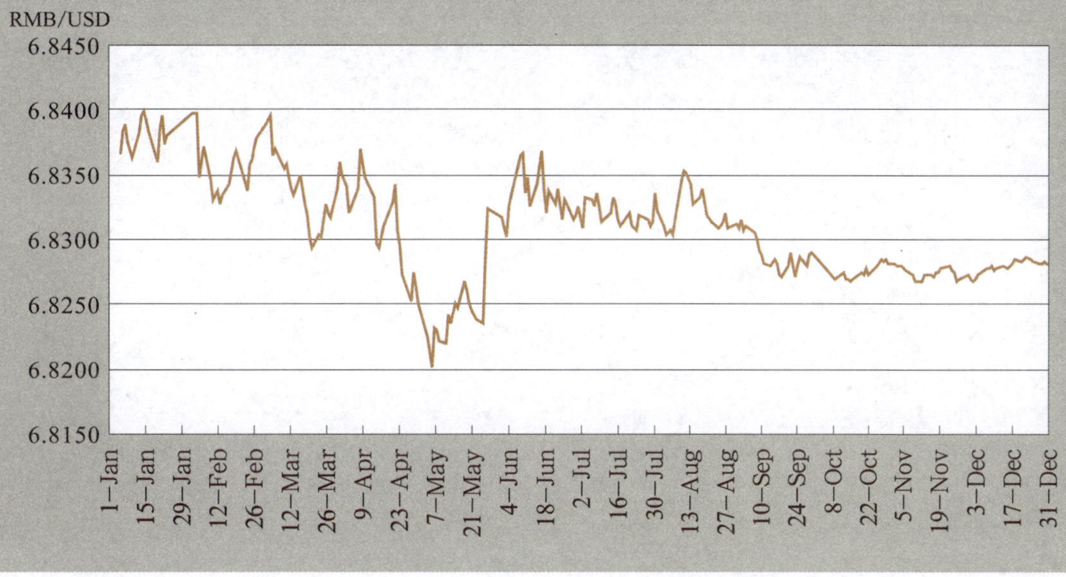

2. RMB/Other major currencies: Either appreciation or depreciation

At the end of 2009, the RMB central parity against the HKD closed at 0.88048, an appreciation of 0.2 percent from 0.88189 at the end of 2008. The RMB central parity against 100 JPY closed at 7.3782, an appreciation of 2.5 percent from 7.5650 at the end of 2008. The RMB central parity against the Euro closed at 9.7971, a depreciation of 1.4 percent from 9.6590 at the end of 2008. The RMB central parity against the GBP closed at 10.9780, a depreciation of 10.0 percent from 9.8798 at the end of 2008.

Chart 3-2

Trends in the RMB/EUR, RMB/JPY, RMB/HKD, and RMB/GBP Central Parity in 2009

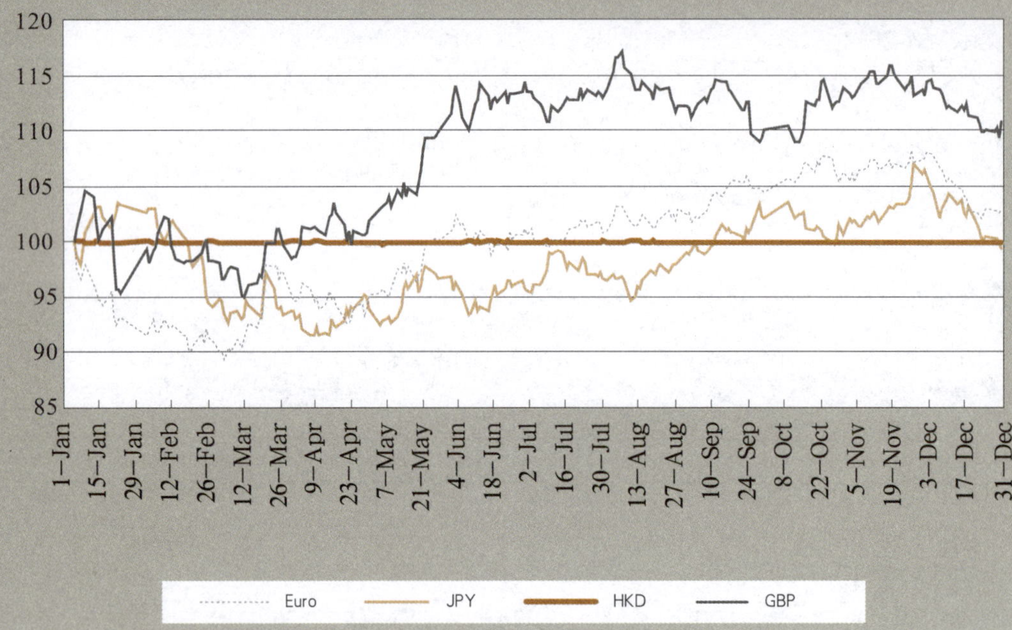

3. The flexibility of the trading price in the inter-bank foreign exchange market decreased

In 2009, the RMB trading price against the USD in the spot inter-bank foreign exchange market floated within a narrow band around the central parity. The daily fluctuation of the trading price over the central parity hit a peak of 0.04 percent, after having been 0.15 percent in 2008. The average daily floating band (the highest price minus the lowest price) reached 29bps, down 82 bps from 2008.

4. Expectations regarding the RMB exchange rate in both domestic and overseas markets changed from depreciation to appreciation

In 2009, RMB forward rates against USD in both the domestic and overseas markets first witnessed a depreciation, followed by an appreciation, which was obviously strengthened in the second half of 2009. In the first quarter, RMB forward rate against USD maintained a premium, revealing some expectations for a depreciation of RMB. The top one-year NDF premium in the overseas market exceeded 2 500 bps, which means RMB exchange rate was expected to depreciate by nearly 4 percent, whereas the premium of the domestic forward rate was far lower. After late March, because USD weakened in the international market, RMB forward rate became stronger in both the domestic and overseas markets. From April, the NDF in the overseas market changed, leading to expectations for an appreciation of RMB, whereas the domestic forward rate exhibited in succession a premium and then a discount. After late September, as the Chinese economy was continuing to become robust, the domestic forward rate developed into expectations for an appreciation and this trend was maintained until 2009, with expectations for an appreciation of the one-year forward rate in the domestic and overseas markets reaching 2.5 percent and 4 percent respectively.

Chart 3-3

USD Discount/Premium of 1-Year Domestic and Overseas Forward Exchange Rate in 2009

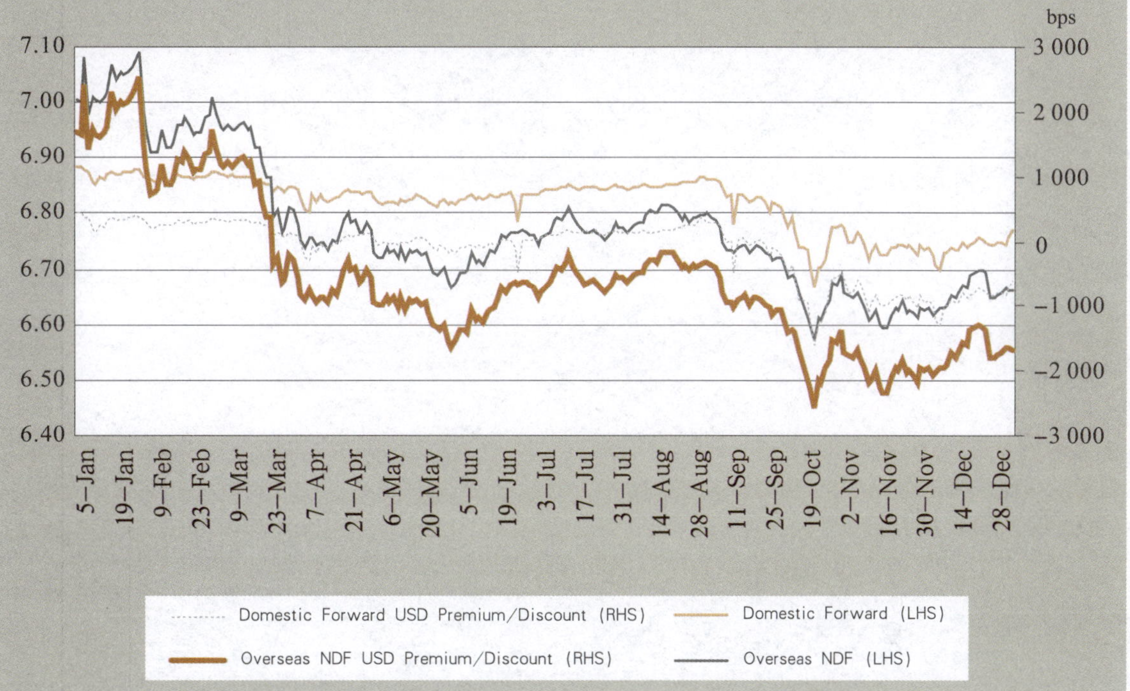

5. The RMB effective exchange rate exhibited relatively high volatility

Since 2009, due to the fact that the central parity of the RMB remained basically stable, the RMB effective exchange rate (the multilateral exchange rate) has followed the trend of the USD in the international market, first appreciating and then depreciating. From the BIS data, in the first three consecutive months of 2009, the RMB nominal effective exchange rate index continued to increase, appreciating by 4.1 percent. In the following eight months, the nominal effective exchange rate index decreased, reaching 111.68 at the end of December, depreciating by 5.4 percent from the end of 2008, appreciating by 12.7 percent from the pre–regime reform in June 2005, and appreciating by 3.3 percent from June 2008 when the financial crisis first erupted. The real effective exchange rate index after deducting for inflation exhibited a similar trend. It appreciated by 4 percent in the first two months, continued to depreciate in the following five months, rebounded a bit to appreciate in August, and then depreciated again . The real effective exchange rate index reached 113.78 at the end of December, depreciating by 6.1 percent from the end of 2008, appreciating by 16.3 percent from the pre–regime reform in June 2005, and appreciating by 3.4 percent from June 2008.

Chart 3–4

The RMB Effective Exchange Rate from Jan. 1994 to Dec. 2009

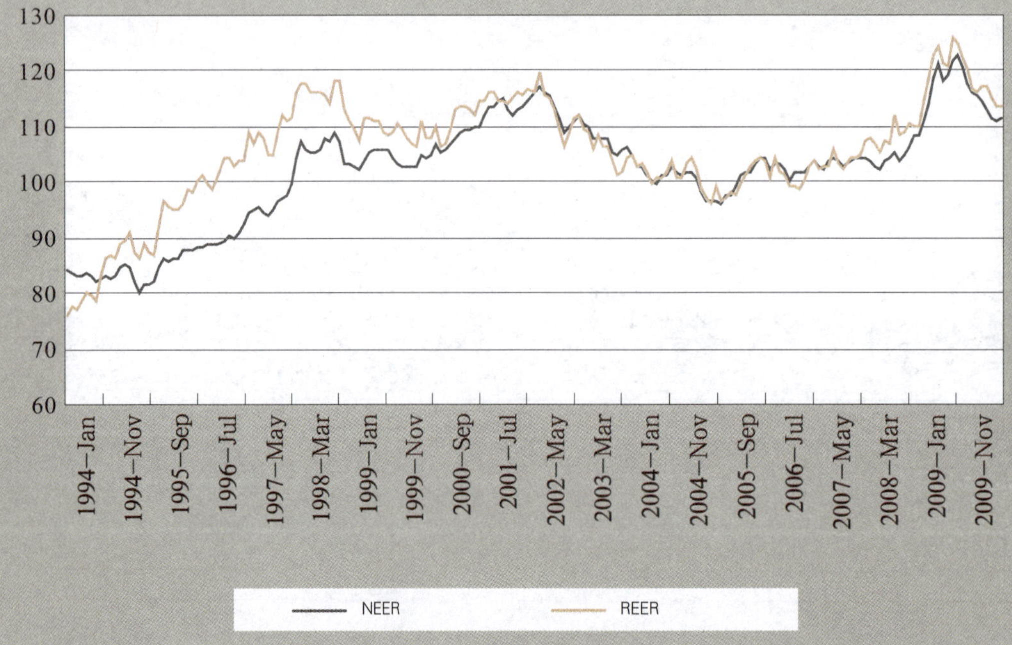

(Ⅲ) Transactions in the Inter–bank Foreign Exchange Market

1. The inter–bank foreign exchange spot transactions

As the global financial market stabilized and net settlement for OTC transactions in the inter–bank foreign exchange market was launched, the market began to recover in 2009, and transactions exceeded the level before the international financial crisis in 2008. The total trading volume in the spot inter–bank foreign exchange market increased by 19.3 percent from 2008, with a rise in the daily trading volume of 20.3 percent. The OTC mode still dominated the spot foreign exchange market, with the proportion of the OTC mode and the automatic price–matching mode standing at 249:1.

2. Inter–bank foreign exchange forward transactions

In 2009, there were 2 501 inter–bank foreign exchange forward transactions and a total trading volume of USD 9.767 billion, with a daily trading volume of USD 40 million. The total and daily trading volume declined by 43.8 percent and 43.3 percent respectively.

Chart 3-5

Trading Volume of the Inter-bank Foreign Exchange Forward and Swap Transactions from Jan. 2007 to Dec. 2009

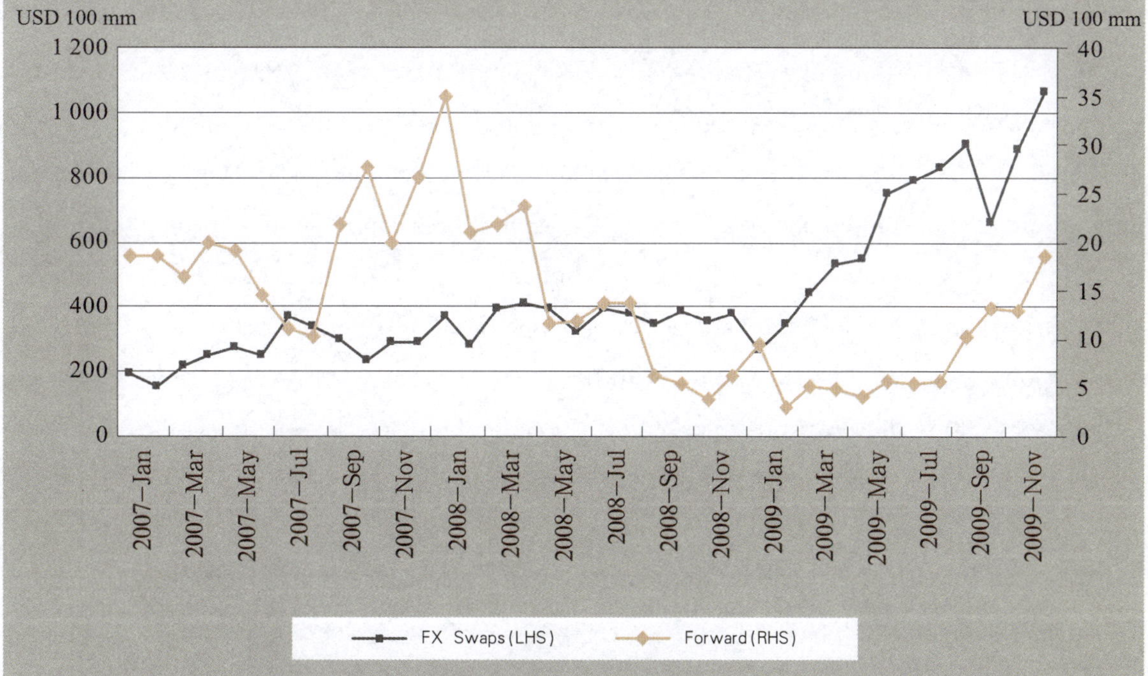

3. Inter–bank foreign exchange swap transactions

In 2009, there were 30 708 inter–bank foreign exchange swap transactions and a total trading volume of USD 801.802 billion, with a daily trading volume of USD 3.286 billion. The total and daily trading volume increased by 82.1 percent and 83.6 percent respectively.

4. Inter–bank foreign currency transactions

By the end of 2009, there were 16 market–maker banks and 84 market–participant banks in the inter–bank foreign currency market. There were 31 620 transactions and a total trading volume of USD 34.786 billion for the spot transactions of the 8 foreign currency pairs, with a daily trading volume of USD 143 million, down 43.3 percent from 2008.

Table 3-1 Foreign Currency Transactions in the Inter-bank Market in 2009

Currency Pair	EUR/USD	AUD/USD	GBP/USD	USD/JPY	USD/CAD	USD/CHF	USD/HKD	EUR/JPY
Trading Volume (USD 100 million)	98.77	8.88	29.30	23.40	11.74	3.46	168.94	3.38
Percentage (%)	28.4	2.6	8.4	6.7	3.4	1.0	48.6	1.0
Percentage Increase YoY (%)	-59.4	80.9	-8.3	-69.2	-22.5	-18.4	-29.1	-50.2
Deals	14 648	2 099	2 786	4 585	720	332	5 683	767

Note: Trading volume is given in USD denominated amounts.

5. The liquidity and efficiency of the foreign exchange market improved

In 2009, the market–maker system continued to play an active role in maintaining market liquidity. The trading volume of the market makers increased steadily, which accelerated a bit more quickly than the total trading volume of the market, accounting for 90.2 percent of the total trading volume of the market and representing an increase of 2.7 percent from 2008. With the support of the automatic pricing system, the speed of the reaction of the market makers continued to be greater for their transaction orders in 2009. The narrowest bilateral effective pricing points was reduced to 2.7 bps, with the average pricing points of the market makers standing at 4.2 bps, down 6.4 bps from 2008.

Ⅳ. BOP Outlook and Policy Orientation

(I) Outlook

From the international perspective, the global economy is expected to continue to recover in 2010. The emerging market countries will lead global economic growth, and the advanced economies will emerge from the recession and recover. Large economic stimulus packages and strengthened policy coordination are helping to restore confidence. Cross-border capital flows will move more rapidly, financial market transactions will be more active, and systemic risks in the financial system will be reduced. According to the projections of the IMF in January 2010, the global economy will grow at 3.9 percent, representing more rapid growth than that in 2008. Meanwhile, the crisis will still have broad and long-lasting effects. Global economic and financial stability will still face many challenges. The high unemployment rate, huge fiscal deficit and government debt, uncertainty about the end of the stimulus packages, trade and investment protectionism, and other lasting effects of the crisis will interact with one another, which may produce unstable economic fundamentals. The stability of the financial system is still not very solid, and recovery of credit extensions and repairing the balance sheets of financial institutions will require more time. As the governments' bailout efforts are easing, we need to pay closer attention to the respective risks of some large institutions. The speed of the economic recovery varies between the U.S. and the Euro area. Some Euro area countries are facing huge fiscal deficits, poor financing abilities, and high sovereign debt risks, which may affect global economic and financial stability.

From the domestic perspective, the Chinese economy will continue to grow relatively rapidly in 2010, which will make it a highlight of the global economic recovery. China is accelerating the transformation of its pattern of economic development and economic restructuring and domestic demand will play a more important role in boosting economic growth. On the one hand, China will continue to implement a proactive fiscal policy and keep government spending at a certain level to improve the people's well-being. Under the moderately loose monetary policy, and in light of the more active economic activities and more favorable policies, private investment is expected to increase. On the other hand, China is putting more efforts into encouraging private consumption. Policy measures such as adjusting the allocation of the national income, improving the social safety net, and promoting urban and rural consumption are helping to promote domestic consumption. However, the Chinese economy is still facing some unresolved economic issues and many uncertainties in the global economic and financial environments. It is also facing substantial difficulties in transforming its pattern of economic growth and restructuring. Managing inflation expectations and stabilizing price levels are also prominent tasks ahead.

In summary, the internal and external economic environment will generally stabilize in 2010. Balance of payments transactions are becoming more active. The growth rate of the total volume of balance of payments transactions may exceed that of the domestic economy. After two years of decline in 2008 and 2009, the ratio of the total volume of balance of payments transactions to GDP may increase in 2010. In addition, the surplus in the balance of payments will be relatively large in 2010. With an early economic recovery, relatively abundant investment opportunities, and competitive factor prices, including labor prices, inflows of direct investment from multinational corporations will increase. A comparatively high interest rate and a stronger expectation of a RMB appreciation will also induce more cross-border capital arbitrage transactions. Nevertheless, with more favorable fundamentals for an equilibrium in the balance of payments, the Chinese balance of payments situation is expected to improve in 2010. The trend of an enlarging current account surplus is easing and the ratio of the current account surplus to GDP may further decrease. Along with more direct investments abroad by domestic enterprises, capital outflows will increase. In the medium and long term, China's policy to transform the pattern of its economic growth and to restructure the economy will lay a foundation for an equilibrium in the balance of payments situation.

Box VI

Risks in the Post-Crisis Period

Since 2009, driven by the large stimulus policies, the global economy and financial systems have gradually emerged from the serious situation caused by the international financial crisis and have shown positive signs of stabilization and recovery. In the meantime, some local and individual risks have occurred from time to time. These events, which not only relate to credit risks in the real economy, but also to sovereign risks, have affected the process of economic recovery and financial stabilization of related countries and even the entire world.

The financial crisis of the U.S. automobile industry: At the beginning of 2009, along with the deepening of the international financial crisis, the real economy was affected and private consumption dropped significantly. The automobile market shrunk sharply, and the financing channels for the automobile industry were blocked. Large U.S. car manufacturers suffered from a shortage of cash flows. Restructuring was needed. After General Motors, Ford Motor, and Chrysler all encountered trouble, the U.S. government implemented some measures, including funding assistance, car purchase subsidies, and so forth, to three big automakers, but the results were limited. In the middle of 2009, both Chrysler and General Motors went through rapid bankruptcy procedures and completed restructuring. In particular, Chrysler sold its good assets to a group comprised of the Automobile Manufacturers' Association, Fiat, the U.S. government, and the Canadian government; General Motors sold its good assets to a new General Motors company of which the U.S. government holds 60.8 percent.

Default of Dubai World: Affected by the financial crisis, the real estate, tourism, trade, financing, and other pillar industries of Dubai were all in trouble. As a result, Dubai World, Dubai's largest state-owned company, which was highly leveraged and loaded with debt of USD 59 billion, suffered from a breakdown in its funding chain. It announced in November that reimbursement of the debts of its subsidiary Nakheel was postponed to after May 30, 2010. Debt holders were asked to accept this postponement. After the Abu Dhabi government and the UAE central bank announced bailout policies, and Dubai World and its creditors made progress in debt restructuring negotiations, and the impact of the default on global markets, especially emerging markets, gradually dissipated. By the beginning of February 2010, the Dubai government had injected USD 6.2 billion into Dubai World.

The downgrading of the Greek sovereign rating: At the end of 2009, because of a high fiscal deficit, huge government debt, and the government's failure to respond effectively, Greece suffered from a downgrading of its sovereign rating by the three rating agencies including Fitch, Standard & Poor's, and Moody's, rendering it the first country in the Euro area under A-minus. The downgrading sharply raised the Greek government bond spread. It also intensified worries by market participants about the sovereign debt risks of the Euro area countries that were also facing problems of a high deficit, huge debt, low growth, and a weak banking system. The rating agencies gave Ireland, Spain, and Portugal negative ratings in succession and the government bond yield spreads in these three countries climbed sharply. A common concern in the market was that the increase in the sovereign debt risks in the Euro area might have a series of effects that will drag down the economic recovery in the region.

In addition, the veto by the president of Iceland president to the reimbursement act for British and Dutch depositors, the bankruptcy and restructuring of JAL, the largest airline of Asia, and CIT, the biggest commercial loan institution for small and medium-sized companies in the U.S., also had differing degrees of impacts on economic and financial markets.

These post-crisis risks represent warnings that in the process of extricating from their serious situations, economic and financial markets will still be affected by the broad and lasting effects of the crisis. There are still many risks and uncertainties in the real economy and financial markets. In particular, those countries, regions, and issuing entities that have heavy debt burdens are still prone to default or shocks. We need to pay closer attention to the individual and partial risks in the economic and financial markets.

(II) Policy Orientation

In 2010, the foreign exchange administration agencies will fully implement the overall macro-management plan established by the government, work toward the strategic goal of transforming the economic growth model and adjusting the economic structure, continue to transform the foreign exchange administration principles and methods, and promote reforms in important areas of foreign exchange administration. On the premise that the risks are under control, the foreign exchange administration agencies will provide facilitation for economic entities, by gradually reducing prior approval and administration and strengthening post monitoring and analysis. During the next stage, the foreign exchange administration agencies will focus on strengthening supervision of abnormal cross-border capital flows, increase transparency of foreign exchange policies, improve management of foreign exchange reserves, and promote an equilibrium in the balance of payments. Specifically, the following measures will be taken:

First, the foreign exchange administration agencies will promote reforms in important areas of foreign exchange administration. They will push forward the reforms in some important areas and in critical links, including the verification for import payments and export receipts, management of foreign exchange accounts, widening of capital outflow channels, and standardization of domestic foreign exchange market development, with the aim of promoting the rapid development of the external economy. Second, they will improve the monitoring and supervision of abnormal cross-border capital flows. They will establish and improve monitoring and early-warning, off-site inspection, and the emergency management system, improve foreign exchange management of trade credit, trade in services, and external guarantees, and strengthen crackdowns on illegal activities, including underground banks. They will also diversify foreign exchange policy tools and prevent and resolve risks associated with the movement of cross-border capital. Third, they will further increase the transparency of foreign exchange policies. They will promote the revision of the *Regulations on Statistics and Reporting of the Balance of Payments*, enlarge the scope of disclosure of balance of payments statistics, strengthen consolidation of foreign exchange regulations, improve communications with the media and the public, and make timely explanations to highlight issues of foreign exchange administration. Fourth, they will further improve management of foreign exchange reserves and ensure the safety and profitability of foreign exchange reserves.

附 录 统计资料
Appendix Statistics

一、国际收支①

I. Balance of Payments

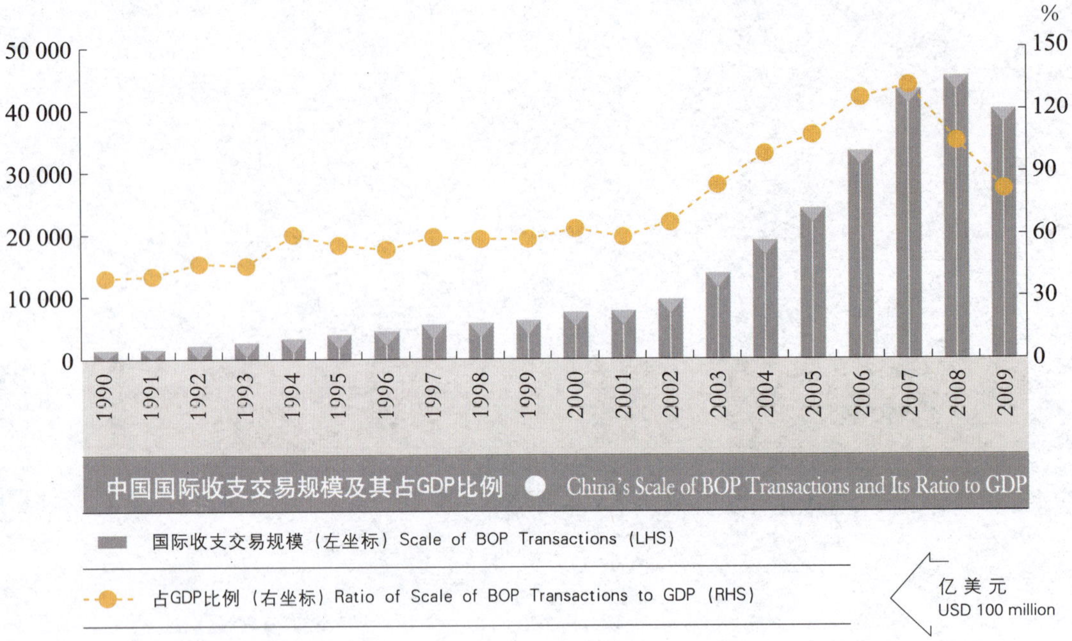

中国国际收支交易规模及其占GDP比例 China's Scale of BOP Transactions and Its Ratio to GDP

①资料来源：国家外汇管理局；IMF：《国际收支统计》、《国际金融统计》；CEIC Asia Database。
Sources: State Administration of Foreign Exchange; IMF, *Balance of Payments Statistics*, *International Financial Statistics*; CEIC Asia Database.

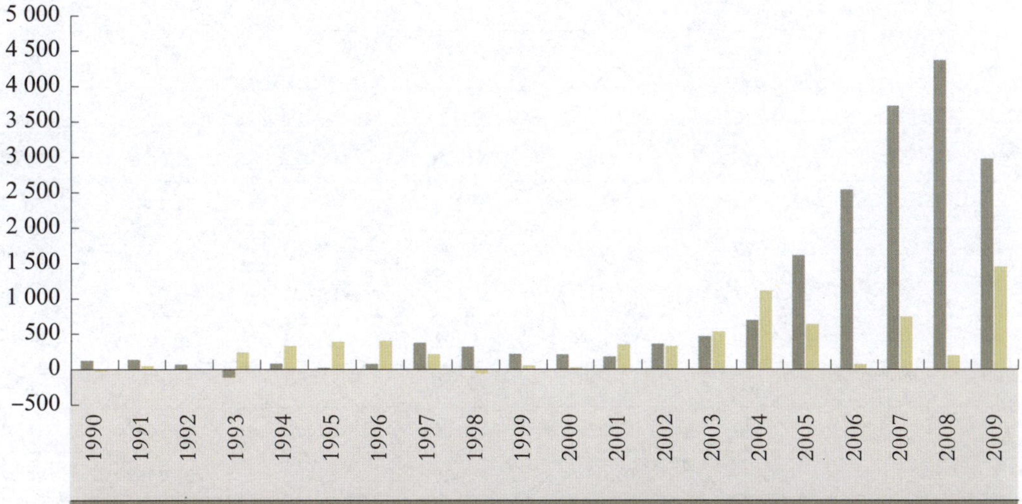

中国经常项目差额与资本和金融项目差额

China's Current Account Balance & Capital and Financial Account Balance

■ 经常项目差额 Current Account Balance

■ 资本和金融项目差额 Capital and Financial Account Balance

亿美元
USD 100 million

中国国际收支概览表（1）

China's Balance of Payments Abridged

单位：百万美元
Unit: USD million

项目 Item / 年份 Year	1982	1983	1984	1985	1986	1987
一、经常项目差额 Current Account Balance	**5 674**	**4 240**	**2 030**	**−11 417**	**−7 035**	**300**
贷方 Credit	25 401	25 355	29 320	30 078	31 199	40 536
借方 Debit	19 727	21 115	27 290	41 495	38 234	40 236
A.货物和服务差额 Goods and Services Balance	**4 812**	**2 571**	**54**	**−12 501**	**−7 390**	**291**
贷方 Credit	23 712	23 282	26 802	28 253	29 782	39 171
借方 Debit	18 900	20 711	26 748	40 754	37 172	38 880
a.货物差额 Goods Balance	**4 249**	**1 990**	**14**	**−13 123**	**−9 140**	**−1 661**
贷方 Credit	21 125	20 707	23 905	25 108	25 756	34 734
借方 Debit	16 876	18 717	23 891	38 231	34 896	36 395
b.服务差额 Services Balance	**563**	**581**	**40**	**622**	**1 750**	**1 952**
贷方 Credit	2 587	2 575	2 897	3 145	4 026	4 437
借方 Debit	2 024	1 994	2 857	2 523	2 276	2 485
B.收益差额 Income Balance	**376**	**1 158**	**1 534**	**841**	**−23**	**−215**
贷方 Credit	1 017	1 453	1 922	1 387	901	976
借方 Debit	641	295	388	546	924	1 191
C.经常转移差额 Current Transfers Balance	**486**	**511**	**442**	**243**	**378**	**224**
贷方 Credit	672	620	596	438	516	389
借方 Debit	186	109	154	195	138	165
二、资本和金融项目差额 Capital and Financial Account Balance	**−1 736**	**−1 372**	**−3 752**	**8 485**	**6 540**	**2 731**
贷方 Credit	3 556	3 041	4 512	21 174	21 333	19 166
借方 Debit	5 292	4 413	8 264	12 689	14 793	16 435
A.资本账户差额 Capital Account Balance	**0**	**0**	**0**	**0**	**0**	**0**
贷方 Credit	0	0	0	0	0	0
借方 Debit	0	0	0	0	0	0
B.金融账户差额 Financial Account Balance	**−1 736**	**−1 372**	**−3 752**	**8 485**	**6 540**	**2 731**
贷方 Credit	3 556	3 041	4 512	21 174	21 333	19 166
借方 Debit	5 292	4 413	8 264	12 689	14 793	16 435

单位：百万美元
Unit: USD million

项目 Item | 年份 Year	1982	1983	1984	1985	1986	1987
1.直接投资差额 Direct Investment Balance	**386**	**823**	**1 285**	**1 327**	**1 794**	**1 669**
贷方 Credit	430	916	1 419	1 956	2 244	2 314
借方 Debit	44	93	134	629	450	645
2.证券投资差额 Portfolio Investment Balance	**21**	**−621**	**−1 638**	**3 027**	**1 568**	**1 051**
贷方 Credit	41	153	942	3 049	1 608	1 191
借方 Debit	20	774	2 580	22	40	140
3.其他投资差额 Other Investment Balance	**−2 143**	**−1 574**	**−3 399**	**4 131**	**3 178**	**11**
贷方 Credit	3 085	1 972	2 151	16 169	17 481	15 661
借方 Debit	5 228	3 546	5 550	12 038	14 303	15 650
三、储备资产变动额 Reserve Assets	**−4 217**	**−2 695**	**531**	**5 422**	**1 727**	**−1 660**
贷方 Credit	61	0	681	5 576	1 851	0
借方 Debit	4 278	2 695	150	154	124	1 660
其中：外汇储备差额 Foreign Exchange Reserves	−4 278	−1 915	681	5 576	1 172	−1 451
四、净误差与遗漏 Net Errors and Omissions	**279**	**−173**	**1 191**	**−2 490**	**−1 232**	**−1 371**

中国国际收支概览表（2）

China's Balance of Payments Abridged

项目 Item / 年份 Year	1988	1989	1990	1991	1992	1993
一、经常项目差额 Current Account Balance	**−3 803**	**−4 318**	**11 997**	**13 271**	**6 401**	**−11 904**
贷方 Credit	47 949	50 193	60 767	70 507	85 618	92 237
借方 Debit	51 752	54 511	48 770	57 236	79 217	104 141
A.货物和服务差额 Goods and Services Balance	**−4 061**	**−4 928**	**10 668**	**11 601**	**4 998**	**−11 792**
贷方 Credit	45 912	47 822	57 374	65 898	78 817	86 557
借方 Debit	49 973	52 750	46 706	54 297	73 819	98 349
a.货物差额 Goods Balance	**−5 315**	**−5 620**	**9 165**	**8 743**	**5 183**	**−10 654**
贷方 Credit	41 054	43 220	51 519	58 919	69 568	75 659
借方 Debit	46 369	48 840	42 354	50 176	64 385	86 313
b.服务差额 Services Balance	**1 254**	**692**	**1 503**	**2 858**	**−185**	**−1 138**
贷方 Credit	4 858	4 602	5 855	6 979	9 249	10 898
借方 Debit	3 604	3 910	4 352	4 121	9 434	12 036
B.收益差额 Income Balance	**−161**	**229**	**1 055**	**840**	**248**	**−1 284**
贷方 Credit	1 469	1 894	3 017	3 719	5 595	4 390
借方 Debit	1 630	1 665	1 962	2 879	5 347	5 674
C.经常转移差额 Current Transfers Balance	**419**	**381**	**274**	**830**	**1 155**	**1 172**
贷方 Credit	568	477	376	890	1 206	1 290
借方 Debit	149	96	102	60	51	118
二、资本和金融项目差额 Capital and Financial Account Balance	**5 269**	**6 428**	**−2 774**	**4 580**	**−251**	**23 474**
贷方 Credit	20 262	21 185	20 377	20 323	30 223	50 828
借方 Debit	14 993	14 757	23 151	15 743	30 474	27 354
A.资本账户差额 Capital Account Balance	**0**	**0**	**0**	**0**	**0**	**0**
贷方 Credit	0	0	0	0	0	0
借方 Debit	0	0	0	0	0	0
B.金融账户差额 Financial Account Balance	**5 269**	**6 428**	**−2 774**	**4 580**	**−251**	**23 474**
贷方 Credit	20 262	21 185	20 377	20 323	30 223	50 828
借方 Debit	14 993	14 757	23 151	15 743	30 474	27 354

单位：百万美元
Unit: USD million

项目 Item / 年份 Year	1988	1989	1990	1991	1992	1993
1.直接投资差额 Direct Investment Balance	**2 344**	**2 613**	**2 657**	**3 453**	**7 156**	**23 115**
贷方 Credit	3 194	3 393	3 487	4 366	11 156	27 515
借方 Debit	850	780	830	913	4 000	4 400
2.证券投资差额 Portfolio Investment Balance	**876**	**−180**	**−241**	**235**	**−57**	**3 050**
贷方 Credit	1 216	140	0	565	865	5 042
借方 Debit	340	320	241	330	922	1 992
3.其他投资差额 Other Investment Balance	**2 049**	**3 995**	**−5 190**	**892**	**−7 350**	**−2 691**
贷方 Credit	15 852	17 652	16 890	15 392	18 202	18 271
借方 Debit	13 803	13 657	22 080	14 500	25 552	20 962
三、储备资产变动额 Reserve Assets	**−455**	**−2 202**	**−6 089**	**−11 091**	**2 102**	**−1 767**
贷方 Credit	76	55	0	0	2 427	54
借方 Debit	531	2 257	6 089	11 091	325	1 821
其中：外汇储备差额 Foreign Exchange Reserves	−449	−2 178	−5 543	−10 619	2 269	−1 756
四、净误差与遗漏 Net Errors and Omissions	**−1 011**	**92**	**−3 134**	**−6 760**	**−8 252**	**−9 803**

中国国际收支概览表（3）

China's Balance of Payments Abridged

项目 Item / 年份 Year	1994	1995	1996	1997	1998	1999
一、经常项目差额 Current Account Balance	**7 658**	**1 618**	**7 242**	**36 963**	**31 471**	**21 114**
贷方 Credit	126 435	154 257	181 363	218 427	217 670	234 661
借方 Debit	118 777	152 639	174 121	181 464	186 199	213 547
A.货物和服务差额 Goods and Services Balance	**7 357**	**11 958**	**17 550**	**42 823**	**43 837**	**30 641**
贷方 Credit	118 927	147 240	171 677	207 239	207 425	220 964
借方 Debit	111 570	135 282	154 127	164 416	163 589	190 323
a.货物差额 Goods Balance	**7 290**	**18 050**	**19 535**	**46 222**	**46 614**	**35 980**
贷方 Credit	102 561	128 110	151 077	182 670	183 529	194 716
借方 Debit	95 271	110 060	131 542	136 448	136 916	158 735
b.服务差额 Services Balance	**67**	**−6 092**	**−1 985**	**−3 399**	**−2 777**	**−5 339**
贷方 Credit	16 366	19 130	20 600	24 569	23 896	26 248
借方 Debit	16 299	25 222	22 585	27 968	26 673	31 588
B.收益差额 Income Balance	**−1 036**	**−11 774**	**−12 437**	**−11 004**	**−16 644**	**−14 470**
贷方 Credit	5 738	5 191	7 318	5 711	5 584	8 330
借方 Debit	6 774	16 965	19 755	16 715	22 228	22 800
C.经常转移差额 Current Transfers Balance	**1 337**	**1 434**	**2 129**	**5 143**	**4 278**	**4 943**
贷方 Credit	1 770	1 826	2 368	5 477	4 661	5 367
借方 Debit	433	392	239	334	382	424
二、资本和金融项目差额 Capital and Financial Account Balance	**32 644**	**38 675**	**39 967**	**21 015**	**−6 321**	**5 180**
贷方 Credit	61 793	67 712	70 977	92 637	89 327	91 754
借方 Debit	29 149	29 037	31 010	71 622	95 648	86 574
A.资本账户差额 Capital Account Balance	**0**	**0**	**0**	**−21**	**−47**	**−26**
贷方 Credit	0	0	0	0	0	0
借方 Debit	0	0	0	21	47	26
B.金融账户差额 Financial Account Balance	**32 644**	**38 675**	**39 967**	**21 036**	**−6 275**	**5 205**
贷方 Credit	61 793	67 712	70 977	92 637	89 327	91 754
借方 Debit	29 149	29 037	31 010	71 601	95 601	86 549

单位：百万美元
Unit: USD million

项目 Item | 年份 Year	1994	1995	1996	1997	1998	1999
1.直接投资差额 Direct Investment Balance	**31 787**	**33 849**	**38 066**	**41 674**	**41 118**	**36 978**
贷方 Credit	33 787	37 736	42 350	45 439	45 645	41 015
借方 Debit	2 000	3 887	4 284	3 765	4 527	4 037
2.证券投资差额 Portfolio Investment Balance	**3 543**	**790**	**1 744**	**6 942**	**−3 733**	**−11 234**
贷方 Credit	4 493	1 803	3 354	9 230	1 899	1 808
借方 Debit	950	1 013	1 610	2 288	5 632	13 042
3.其他投资差额 Other Investment Balance	**−2 686**	**4 036**	**157**	**−27 580**	**−43 660**	**−20 540**
贷方 Credit	23 513	28 173	25 273	37 968	41 783	48 931
借方 Debit	26 199	24 137	25 116	65 548	85 443	69 470
三、储备资产变动额 Reserve Assets	**−30 527**	**−22 463**	**−31 662**	**−35 724**	**−6 426**	**−8 505**
贷方 Credit	0	0	0	12	0	1 252
借方 Debit	30 527	22 463	31 662	35 736	6 426	9 757
其中：外汇储备差额 Foreign Exchange Reserves	−30 421	−21 959	−31 450	−34 862	−5 069	−9 716
四、净误差与遗漏 Net Errors and Omissions	**−9 775**	**−17 830**	**−15 547**	**−22 254**	**−18 724**	**−17 788**

中国国际收支概览表（4）

China's Balance of Payments Abridged

项目 Item | 年份 Year	2000	2001	2002	2003	2004	2005
一、经常项目差额 Current Account Balance	**20 519**	**17 405**	**35 422**	**45 875**	**68 659**	**160 818**
贷方 Credit	298 973	317 924	387 535	519 580	700 697	903 582
借方 Debit	278 454	300 519	352 113	473 706	632 038	742 763
A.货物和服务差额 Goods and Services Balance	**28 873**	**28 086**	**37 383**	**36 079**	**49 284**	**124 798**
贷方 Credit	279 561	299 410	365 395	485 003	655 827	836 888
借方 Debit	250 688	271 324	328 013	448 924	606 543	712 090
a.货物差额 Goods Balance	**34 474**	**34 017**	**44 167**	**44 652**	**58 982**	**134 189**
贷方 Credit	249 131	266 075	325 651	438 270	593 393	762 484
借方 Debit	214 657	232 058	281 484	393 618	534 410	628 295
b.服务差额 Services Balance	**−5 600**	**−5 931**	**−6 784**	**−8 573**	**−9 699**	**−9 391**
贷方 Credit	30 430	33 335	39 745	46 734	62 434	74 404
借方 Debit	36 031	39 266	46 528	55 306	72 133	83 795
B.收益差额 Income Balance	**−14 666**	**−19 173**	**−14 945**	**−7 838**	**−3 523**	**10 635**
贷方 Credit	12 551	9 390	8 344	16 095	20 544	38 959
借方 Debit	27 216	28 563	23 289	23 933	24 067	28 324
C.经常转移差额 Current Transfers Balance	**6 311**	**8 492**	**12 984**	**17 634**	**22 898**	**25 385**
贷方 Credit	6 861	9 125	13 795	18 482	24 326	27 735
借方 Debit	550	632	811	848	1 428	2 349
二、资本和金融项目差额 Capital and Financial Account Balance	**1 922**	**34 775**	**32 291**	**52 726**	**110 660**	**62 964**
贷方 Credit	91 986	99 531	128 321	219 631	343 350	418 956
借方 Debit	90 064	64 756	96 030	166 905	232 690	355 992
A.资本账户差额 Capital Account Balance	**−35**	**−54**	**−50**	**−48**	**−69**	**4 102**
贷方 Credit	0	0	0	0	0	4 155
借方 Debit	35	54	50	48	69	53
B.金融账户差额 Financial Account Balance	**1 958**	**34 829**	**32 340**	**52 774**	**110 729**	**58 862**
贷方 Credit	91 986	99 531	128 321	219 631	343 350	414 801
借方 Debit	90 029	64 702	95 981	166 857	232 621	355 939

单位：百万美元
Unit: USD million

项目 Item | 年份 Year	2000	2001	2002	2003	2004	2005
1.直接投资差额 Direct Investment Balance	**37 483**	**37 356**	**46 790**	**47 229**	**53 131**	**67 821**
贷方 Credit	42 096	47 052	53 074	55 507	60 906	86 071
借方 Debit	4 613	9 697	6 284	8 278	7 774	18 250
2.证券投资差额 Portfolio Investment Balance	**−3 991**	**−19 406**	**−10 342**	**11 427**	**19 690**	**−4 933**
贷方 Credit	7 814	2 404	2 287	12 307	20 262	21 997
借方 Debit	11 805	21 810	12 629	880	572	26 930
3.其他投资差额 Other Investment Balance	**−31 535**	**16 879**	**−4 107**	**−5 882**	**37 908**	**−4 026**
贷方 Credit	42 076	50 075	72 961	151 817	262 182	306 732
借方 Debit	73 611	33 196	77 068	157 699	224 274	310 758
三、储备资产变动额 Reserve Assets	**−10 548**	**−47 325**	**−75 507**	**−117 023**	**−206 364**	**−207 016**
贷方 Credit	407	0	0	0	478	1 929
借方 Debit	10 955	47 325	75 507	117 023	206 842	208 945
其中：外汇储备差额 Foreign Exchange Reserves	−10 898	−46 591	−74 242	−116 844	−206 681	−208 940
四、净误差与遗漏 Net Errors and Omissions	**−11 893**	**−4 856**	**7 794**	**18 422**	**27 045**	**−16 766**

中国国际收支概览表（5）

China's Balance of Payments Abridged

项目 Item | 年份 Year	2006	2007	2008	2009
一、经常项目差额 Current Account Balance	**253 268**	**371 833**	**436 107**	**297 142**
贷方 Credit	1 147 901	1 467 882	1 735 893	1 484 573
借方 Debit	894 633	1 096 049	1 299 786	1 187 431
A.货物和服务差额 Goods and Services Balance	**208 912**	**307 477**	**348 870**	**220 112**
贷方 Credit	1 061 682	1 342 206	1 581 713	1 333 346
借方 Debit	852 769	1 034 729	1 232 843	1 113 234
a.货物差额 Goods Balance	**217 746**	**315 381**	**360 682**	**249 509**
贷方 Credit	969 682	1 220 000	1 434 601	1 203 797
借方 Debit	751 936	904 618	1 073 919	954 287
b.服务差额 Services Balance	**−8 834**	**−7 905**	**−11 812**	**−29 398**
贷方 Credit	91 999	122 206	147 112	129 549
借方 Debit	100 833	130 111	158 924	158 947
B.收益差额 Income Balance	**15 156**	**25 688**	**31 438**	**43 282**
贷方 Credit	54 642	83 030	91 615	108 582
借方 Debit	39 485	57 342	60 177	65 299
C.经常转移差额 Current Transfers Balance	**29 199**	**38 668**	**45 799**	**33 748**
贷方 Credit	31 578	42 646	52 565	42 645
借方 Debit	2 378	3 978	6 766	8 897
二、资本和金融项目差额 Capital and Financial Account Balance	**6 662**	**73 509**	**18 965**	**144 828**
贷方 Credit	653 276	921 961	769 876	746 439
借方 Debit	646 614	848 451	750 911	601 611
A.资本账户差额 Capital Account Balance	**4 020**	**3 099**	**3 051**	**3 958**
贷方 Credit	4 102	3 315	3 320	4 204
借方 Debit	82	216	268	247
B.金融账户差额 Financial Account Balance	**2 642**	**70 410**	**15 913**	**140 871**
贷方 Credit	649 174	918 646	766 556	742 235
借方 Debit	646 532	848 236	750 643	601 364

单位：百万美元
Unit: USD million

项目 Item | 年份 Year	2006	2007	2008	2009
1.直接投资差额 Direct Investment Balance	**56 935**	**121 418**	**94 320**	**34 294**
贷方 Credit	87 285	151 554	163 054	114 198
借方 Debit	30 351	30 135	68 734	79 904
2.证券投资差额 Portfolio Investment Balance	**−67 558**	**18 672**	**42 660**	**38 691**
贷方 Credit	45 602	63 969	67 708	98 112
借方 Debit	113 159	45 297	25 048	59 420
3.其他投资差额 Other Investment Balance	**13 265**	**−69 680**	**−121 067**	**67 885**
贷方 Credit	516 287	703 123	535 794	529 925
借方 Debit	503 022	772 803	656 861	462 040
三、储备资产变动额 Reserve Assets	**−246 981**	**−461 744**	**−418 978**	**−398 422**
贷方 Credit	491	240	0	0
借方 Debit	247 472	461 984	418 978	398 422
其中：外汇储备差额 Foreign Exchange Reserves	−247 472	−461 905	−417 781	−382 051
四、净误差与遗漏 Net Errors and Omissions	**−12 949**	**16 402**	**−26 094**	**−43 548**

2009年中国国际收支平衡表

China's Balance of Payments in 2009

项目 Item	差 额 Balance	贷 方 Credit	借 方 Debit
一、经常项目Current Account	**297 142**	**1 484 573**	**1 187 431**
A.货物和服务Goods and Services	**220 112**	**1 333 346**	**1 113 234**
a.货物Goods	**249 509**	**1 203 797**	**954 287**
b.服务Services	**−29 398**	**129 549**	**158 947**
1.运输Transportation	−23 005	23 569	46 574
2.旅游Travel	−4 027	39 675	43 702
3.通讯服务Communication Services	−11	1 198	1 210
4.建筑服务Construction Services	3 595	9 463	5 868
5.保险服务Insurance Services	−9 713	1 596	11 309
6.金融服务Financial Services	−289	437	726
7.计算机和信息服务Computer and Information Services	3 279	6 512	3 233
8.专有权利使用费和特许费Royalties and Licensing Fees	−10 636	429	11 065
9.咨询Consulting Service	5 206	18 623	13 417
10.广告、宣传Advertising and Public Opinion Polling	358	2 313	1 955
11.电影、音像Audio-visual and Related Services	−181	97	278
12.其他商业服务Other Business Services	5 916	24 688	18 772
13.别处未提及的政府服务Government Services, n.i.e	110	950	840
B.收益Income	**43 282**	**108 582**	**65 299**
1.职工报酬Compensation of Employee	7 158	9 209	2 052
2.投资收益Investment Income	36 124	99 372	63 248
C.经常转移Current Transfers	**33 748**	**42 645**	**8 897**
1.各级政府General Government	−247	43	291
2.其他部门Other Sectors	33 996	42 602	8 606
二、资本和金融项目差额Capital and Financial Account Balance	**144 828**	**746 439**	**601 611**
A.资本项目差额Capital Account Balance	**3 958**	**4 204**	**247**
B.金融项目差额Financial Account Balance	**140 871**	**742 235**	**601 364**
1.直接投资差额Direct Investment Balance	**34 294**	**114 198**	**79 904**
1.1 我国在外直接投资Abroad Balance	−43 898	4 163	48 061
1.2 外国在华直接投资In China Balance	78 193	110 036	31 843
2.证券投资差额Portfolio Investment Balance	**38 691**	**98 112**	**59 420**
2.1 资产Assets	9 888	66 919	57 032
2.1.1 股本证券Equity Securities	−33 815	12 241	46 056
2.1.2 债务证券Debt Securities	43 703	54 678	10 976
2.1.2.1 (中)长期债券Bonds and Notes	36 956	47 917	10 961
2.1.2.2 货币市场工具Money Market Instruments	6 747	6 761	14
2.2 负债Liabilities	28 804	31 192	2 389
2.2.1 股本证券Equity Securities	28 161	28 850	689
2.2.2 债务证券Debt Securities	643	2 343	1 700
2.2.2.1 (中)长期债券Bonds and Notes	643	2 342	1 699
2.2.2.2 货币市场工具Money Market Instruments	0	1	1
3.其他投资Other Investment	**67 885**	**529 925**	**462 040**
3.1 资产Assets	9 365	117 394	108 029
3.1.1 贸易信贷Trade Credits	−54 435	0	54 435

单位：百万美元
Unit: USD million

项目 Item	差 额 Balance	贷 方 Credit	借 方 Debit
长期Long-term	-3 810	0	3 810
短期Short-term	-50 625	0	50 625
3.1.2 贷款Loans	12 996	44 962	31 965
长期Long-term	-31 504	0	31 504
短期Short-term	44 500	44 962	461
3.1.3 货币和存款Currency and Deposits	5 171	26 739	21 568
3.1.4 其他资产Other Assets	45 633	45 694	61
长期Long-term	0	0	0
短期Short-term	45 633	45 694	61
3.2 负债Liabilities	58 520	412 531	354 011
3.2.1 贸易信贷Trade Credits	32 058	32 058	0
长期Long-term	2 244	2 244	0
短期Short-term	29 814	29 814	0
3.2.2 贷款Loans	3 749	322 245	318 496
长期Long-term	-9 688	13 495	23 183
短期Short-term	13 437	308 749	295 313
3.2.3 货币和存款Currency and Deposits	11 575	45 622	34 047
3.2.4 其他负债Other Liabilities	11 138	12 606	1 468
长期Long-term	11 029	11 029	0
短期Short-term	109	1 577	1 468
三、储备资产Reserve Assets	**-398 422**	**0**	**398 422**
3.1 货币黄金Monetary Gold	-4 876	0	4 876
3.2 特别提款权Special Drawing Rights	-11 092	0	11 092
3.3 在基金组织的储备头寸Reserve Position in the Fund	-402	0	402
3.4 外汇Foreign Exchange	-382 051	0	382 051
3.5 其他债权Other Claims	0	0	0
四、净误差与遗漏Net Errors and Omissions	**-43 548**	**0**	**43 548**

美国国际收支概览表

Balance of Payments Abridged of United States

项目 Item / 年份 Year	2002	2003	2004	2005	2006	2007	2008	2009
一、经常项目差额 Current Account Balance	**−459.15**	**−521.52**	**−631.13**	**−748.69**	**−803.55**	**−726.57**	**−706.07**	**−419.87**
贷方 Credit	1 270.71	1 355.64	1 593.25	1 835.68	2 159.88	2 485.45	2 613.00	2 135.16
借方 Debit	1 729.86	1 877.16	2 224.38	2 584.37	2 963.42	3 212.02	3 319.06	2 555.04
A.货物和服务差额 Goods and Services Balance	**−421.60**	**−495.04**	**−609.99**	**−715.27**	**−760.36**	**−701.42**	**−695.94**	**−378.64**
贷方 Credit	977.47	1 020.19	1 159.23	1 281.46	1 451.69	1 643.17	1 826.60	1 554.72
借方 Debit	1 399.07	1 515.23	1 769.22	1 996.73	2 212.04	2 344.59	2 522.53	1 933.35
a.货物差额 Goods Balance	**−479.34**	**−545.76**	**−668.38**	**−787.06**	**−843.54**	**−826.91**	**−836.27**	**−512.69**
贷方 Credit	688.68	719.14	809.65	896.16	1 019.56	1 142.47	1 281.01	1 049.95
借方 Debit	1 168.02	1 264.90	1 478.03	1 683.22	1 863.10	1 969.39	2 117.28	1 562.65
b.服务差额 Services Balance	**57.74**	**50.73**	**58.39**	**71.78**	**83.18**	**125.50**	**140.34**	**134.06**
贷方 Credit	288.79	301.05	349.58	385.30	432.13	500.70	545.59	504.77
借方 Debit	231.05	250.33	291.19	313.51	348.94	375.20	405.25	370.70
B.收益差额 Income Balance	**27.40**	**45.31**	**67.22**	**72.36**	**48.09**	**90.84**	**118.23**	**89.00**
贷方 Credit	280.94	320.46	413.74	535.26	682.22	818.93	764.64	561.21
借方 Debit	253.55	275.15	346.52	462.91	634.13	728.09	646.41	472.21
C.经常转移差额 Current Transfers Balance	**−64.95**	**−71.80**	**−88.36**	**−105.77**	**−91.27**	**−116.00**	**−128.36**	**−130.24**
贷方 Credit	12.30	14.99	20.28	18.96	25.98	23.35	21.76	19.24
借方 Debit	77.24	86.79	108.64	124.74	117.25	139.35	150.12	149.48
二、资本和金融项目差额 Capital and Financial Account Balance	**499.04**	**529.41**	**533.65**	**712.07**	**805.26**	**661.66**	**506.02**	**226.07**
A.资本账户差额 Capital Account Balance	**−1.47**	**−3.48**	**1.32**	**11.34**	**−3.91**	**−1.90**	**0.95**	**−2.86**

单位：10亿美元
Unit: USD billion

项目 Item | 年份 Year	2002	2003	2004	2005	2006	2007	2008	2009
B.金融账户差额 **Financial Account Balance**	**500.51**	**532.89**	**532.33**	**700.72**	**809.17**	**663.55**	**505.07**	**228.93**
1.直接投资差额 **Direct Investment Balance**	**−70.09**	**−85.81**	**−170.26**	**76.40**	**−1.77**	**−122.84**	**−12.28**	**−68.89**
1.1本国对外直接投资差额 Abroad Balance	−154.46	−149.56	−316.22	−36.24	−244.92	−398.60	−332.01	−220.97
1.2外国对内直接投资差额 In United States Balance	84.37	63.75	145.97	112.64	243.15	275.76	319.74	152.08
2.证券投资差额 **Portfolio Investment Balance**	**379.04**	**427.03**	**689.98**	**574.50**	**627.84**	**758.70**	**645.07**	**−172.82**
2.1证券投资资产差额 Assets Balance	−48.57	−123.13	−177.36	−257.54	−498.90	−396.01	117.37	−549.39
2.2证券投资负债差额 Liabilities Balance	427.61	550.16	867.34	832.04	1 126.74	1 154.71	527.69	376.57
3.金融衍生工具差额 **Financial Derivatives Balance**	—	—	—	—	**29.71**	**6.22**	**−28.91**	**31.17**
4.其他投资差额 **Other Investment Balance**	**195.24**	**190.14**	**9.81**	**35.72**	**151.00**	**21.59**	**−93.98**	**491.65**
4.1其他投资资产差额 Other Assets Balance	−87.94	−54.26	−510.09	−266.96	−544.28	−677.40	219.38	585.17
4.2其他投资负债差额 Other Liabilities Balance	283.18	244.39	519.90	302.67	695.28	698.99	−313.36	−93.51
5.储备资产差额 **Reserve Assets Balance**	**−3.69**	**1.53**	**2.80**	**14.10**	**2.39**	**−0.13**	**−4.84**	**−52.18**
其中：外汇储备差额 Foreign Exchange Reserves Balance	−0.57	−0.57	−0.62	−0.62	−0.73	−0.99	−1.27	−0.67
三、净误差与遗漏 **Net Errors and Omissions**	**−39.88**	**−7.88**	**97.48**	**36.62**	**−1.71**	**64.91**	**200.04**	**193.80**

德国国际收支概览表

Balance of Payments Abridged of Germany

项目 Item / 年份 Year	2002	2003	2004	2005	2006	2007	2008	2009
一、经常项目差额 Current Account Balance	**41.11**	**46.93**	**128.00**	**142.77**	**189.12**	**254.56**	**246.06**	**168.02**
贷方 Credit	828.06	1 007.28	1 244.56	1 370.52	1 607.19	1 932.48	2 099.60	1 631.96
借方 Debit	786.96	960.35	1 116.56	1 227.76	1 418.07	1 677.92	1 853.55	1 463.94
A.货物和服务差额 Goods and Services Balance	**83.75**	**95.55**	**136.78**	**148.17**	**166.59**	**238.48**	**235.12**	**164.87**
贷方 Credit	714.99	871.24	1 055.29	1 149.74	1 330.95	1 579.53	1 748.67	1 375.82
借方 Debit	631.24	775.69	918.51	1 001.56	1 164.36	1 341.05	1 513.55	1 210.96
a.货物差额 Goods Balance	**125.76**	**144.74**	**186.04**	**193.14**	**198.05**	**270.62**	**265.10**	**188.13**
贷方 Credit	611.84	747.37	907.79	983.14	1 136.16	1 350.37	1 487.30	1 144.56
借方 Debit	486.09	602.63	721.76	790.00	938.11	1 079.75	1 222.21	956.43
b.服务差额 Services Balance	**−42.01**	**−49.19**	**−49.26**	**−44.97**	**−31.46**	**−32.14**	**−29.97**	**−23.26**
贷方 Credit	103.14	123.87	147.50	166.59	194.79	229.16	261.37	231.26
借方 Debit	145.15	173.06	196.76	211.56	226.25	261.30	291.34	254.52
B.收益差额 Income Balance	**−17.02**	**−16.99**	**25.60**	**30.84**	**56.43**	**59.97**	**61.43**	**47.35**
贷方 Credit	97.98	118.53	170.23	200.02	251.69	327.98	323.81	232.30
借方 Debit	115.01	135.52	144.63	169.18	195.26	268.00	262.38	184.95
C.经常转移差额 Current Transfers Balance	**−25.62**	**−31.63**	**−34.38**	**−36.25**	**−33.89**	**−43.89**	**−50.50**	**−44.20**
贷方 Credit	15.09	17.50	19.04	20.77	24.55	24.98	27.12	23.84
借方 Debit	40.71	49.14	53.42	57.01	58.45	68.87	77.63	68.04
二、资本和金融项目差额 Capital and Financial Account Balance	**−39.00**	**−70.57**	**−150.65**	**−163.64**	**−218.43**	**−302.10**	**−292.04**	**−198.54**
A.资本账户差额 Capital Account Balance	**−0.23**	**0.35**	**0.52**	**−1.82**	**−0.34**	**0.08**	**−0.18**	**−0.31**

单位：10亿美元
Unit: USD billion

项目 Item | 年份 Year	2002	2003	2004	2005	2006	2007	2008	2009
B.金融账户差额 Financial Account Balance	**-38.78**	**-70.93**	**-151.17**	**-161.82**	**-218.09**	**-302.18**	**-291.86**	**-198.23**
1.直接投资差额 Direct Investment Balance	**33.98**	**25.78**	**-29.76**	**-30.48**	**-62.57**	**-86.39**	**-112.22**	**-25.75**
1.1本国对外直接投资差额 Abroad Balance	-19.63	-5.15	-19.96	-76.96	-119.22	-163.69	-137.18	-61.59
1.2外国对内直接投资差额 In Germany Balance	53.61	30.93	-9.80	46.47	56.64	77.30	24.95	35.84
2.证券投资差额 Portfolio Investment Balance	**63.52**	**60.60**	**19.25**	**-35.66**	**-22.37**	**201.26**	**48.08**	**-127.61**
2.1证券投资资产差额 Assets Balance	-57.85	-52.51	-128.60	-257.33	-203.39	-199.94	23.07	-101.57
2.2证券投资负债差额 Liabilities Balance	121.37	113.10	147.85	221.66	181.03	401.20	25.01	-26.04
3.金融衍生工具差额 Financial Derivatives Balance	**-1.14**	**-2.38**	**-9.37**	**-12.02**	**-7.77**	**-118.54**	**-40.99**	**26.00**
4.其他投资差额 Other Investment Balance	**-137.11**	**-155.61**	**-133.09**	**-86.25**	**-129.03**	**-297.29**	**-183.98**	**-58.50**
4.1其他投资资产差额 Other Assets Balance	-164.86	-170.90	-179.47	-161.90	-259.54	-455.27	-219.50	135.52
4.2其他投资负债差额 Other Liabilities Balance	27.76	15.30	46.37	75.64	130.50	157.99	35.51	-194.02
5.储备资产差额 Reserve Assets Balance	**1.98**	**0.68**	**1.81**	**2.60**	**3.65**	**-1.23**	**-2.74**	**-12.36**
其中：外汇储备差额 Foreign Exchange Reserves Balance	2.32	0.76	0.75	-0.31	2.02	-1.82	-1.65	5.84
三、净误差与遗漏 Net Errors and Omissions	**-2.10**	**23.64**	**22.65**	**20.87**	**29.31**	**47.54**	**45.98**	**30.52**

英国国际收支概览表

Balance of Payments Abridged of United Kingdom

项目 Item | 年份 Year	2002	2003	2004	2005	2006	2007	2008	2009
一、经常项目差额 Current Account Balance	**−27.86**	**−30.00**	**−45.41**	**−59.41**	**−80.88**	**−74.73**	**−39.90**	**−28.69**
贷方 Credit	618.13	689.22	826.97	962.36	1 156.94	1 339.52	1 281.86	894.19
借方 Debit	645.99	719.22	872.39	1 021.76	1 237.82	1 414.25	1 321.77	922.88
A.货物和服务差额 Goods and Services Balance	**−46.49**	**−48.09**	**−63.66**	**−79.88**	**−78.47**	**−96.55**	**−88.83**	**−57.77**
贷方 Credit	415.17	466.41	547.38	591.99	684.99	727.08	756.48	593.02
借方 Debit	461.66	514.50	611.04	671.87	763.46	823.63	845.30	650.79
a.货物差额 Goods Balance	**−71.77**	**−79.45**	**−111.49**	**−124.73**	**−140.66**	**−179.74**	**−173.93**	**−127.62**
贷方 Credit	279.87	307.80	349.65	384.32	447.59	442.28	467.33	356.40
借方 Debit	351.64	387.25	461.14	509.04	588.25	622.02	641.26	484.03
b.服务差额 Services Balance	**25.29**	**31.37**	**47.83**	**44.84**	**62.19**	**83.19**	**85.10**	**69.85**
贷方 Credit	135.31	158.62	197.73	207.67	237.40	284.80	289.14	236.62
借方 Debit	110.02	127.25	149.90	162.83	175.21	201.61	204.04	166.76
B.收益差额 Income Balance	**31.88**	**34.09**	**37.07**	**42.11**	**19.42**	**48.92**	**75.37**	**51.70**
贷方 Credit	184.55	203.11	254.37	338.70	437.95	584.31	495.31	274.76
借方 Debit	152.66	169.02	217.31	296.59	418.53	535.39	419.94	223.06
C.经常转移差额 Current Transfers Balance	**−13.26**	**−16.00**	**−18.82**	**−21.63**	**−21.83**	**−27.10**	**−26.45**	**−22.62**
贷方 Credit	18.41	19.70	25.22	31.66	34.01	28.13	30.08	26.41
借方 Debit	31.67	35.70	44.04	53.29	55.84	55.23	56.53	49.03
二、资本和金融项目差额 Capital and Financial Account Balance	**38.32**	**39.83**	**57.20**	**53.71**	**72.64**	**68.79**	**30.62**	**34.24**
A.资本账户差额 Capital Account Balance	**1.42**	**2.42**	**3.78**	**2.83**	**1.81**	**5.17**	**6.05**	**5.68**

单位：10亿美元
Unit: USD billion

项目 Item | 年份 Year	2002	2003	2004	2005	2006	2007	2008	2009
B.金融账户差额 Financial Account Balance	**36.90**	**37.40**	**53.42**	**50.89**	**70.84**	**63.61**	**24.56**	**28.56**
1.直接投资差额 Direct Investment Balance	**−24.80**	**−38.02**	**−36.61**	**96.62**	**68.50**	**−77.74**	**−69.64**	**30.29**
1.1本国对外直接投资差额 Abroad Balance	−50.33	−65.64	−93.95	−80.79	−85.62	−275.50	−163.15	−16.70
1.2外国对内直接投资差额 In United Kingdom Balance	25.53	27.61	57.33	177.41	154.12	197.77	93.51	46.99
2.证券投资差额 Portfolio Investment Balance	**75.54**	**114.37**	**−81.15**	**−36.38**	**28.54**	**227.11**	**563.51**	**42.88**
2.1证券投资资产差额 Assets Balance	1.22	−58.42	−259.45	−273.41	−256.99	−179.56	199.63	−241.07
2.2证券投资负债差额 Liabilities Balance	74.32	172.79	178.30	237.04	285.54	406.67	363.88	283.95
3.金融衍生工具差额 Financial Derivatives Balance	**1.35**	**−8.49**	**−14.27**	**16.53**	**14.48**	**−38.08**	**−59.41**	**23.04**
4.其他投资差额 Other Investment Balance	**−15.83**	**−33.04**	**185.86**	**−24.15**	**−41.98**	**−45.11**	**−412.97**	**−58.09**
4.1其他投资资产差额 Other Assets Balance	−108.54	−420.93	−595.88	−926.19	−708.26	−1 484.29	999.98	499.79
4.2其他投资负债差额 Other Liabilities Balance	92.70	387.89	781.74	902.05	666.27	1 439.17	−1 412.95	−557.88
5.储备资产差额 Reserve Assets Balance	**0.63**	**2.59**	**−0.41**	**−1.73**	**1.30**	**−2.57**	**3.07**	**−9.56**
其中：外汇储备差额 Foreign Exchange Reserves Balance	0.79	1.80	−1.53	−3.97	−0.16	−3.04	4.06	5.04
三、净误差与遗漏 Net Errors and Omissions	**−10.46**	**−9.82**	**−11.78**	**5.69**	**8.24**	**5.94**	**9.29**	**−5.55**

日本国际收支概览表

Balance of Payments Abridged of Japan

项目 Item / 年份 Year	2002	2003	2004	2005	2006	2007	2008	2009
一、经常项目差额 Current Account Balance	**112.45**	**136.22**	**172.06**	**165.78**	**170.52**	**210.49**	**156.63**	**142.19**
贷方 Credit	562.81	628.46	756.85	828.58	905.10	1 013.44	1 116.43	858.35
借方 Debit	450.36	492.24	584.79	662.80	734.58	802.95	959.80	716.16
A.货物和服务差额 Goods and Services Balance	**51.60**	**72.49**	**94.23**	**69.91**	**63.05**	**83.50**	**17.34**	**23.25**
贷方 Credit	461.29	526.74	636.61	677.78	733.11	807.21	895.23	673.62
借方 Debit	409.69	454.25	542.38	607.87	670.07	723.70	877.89	650.36
a.货物差额 Goods Balance	**93.83**	**106.40**	**132.13**	**93.96**	**81.30**	**104.75**	**38.13**	**43.63**
贷方 Credit	395.58	449.12	539.00	567.57	615.81	678.09	746.47	545.28
借方 Debit	301.75	342.72	406.87	473.61	534.51	573.34	708.34	501.65
b.服务差额 Services Balance	**−42.23**	**−33.91**	**−37.90**	**−24.05**	**−18.26**	**−21.25**	**−20.79**	**−20.38**
贷方 Credit	65.71	77.62	97.61	110.21	117.30	129.12	148.76	128.34
借方 Debit	107.94	111.53	135.51	134.26	135.56	150.37	169.54	148.72
B.收益差额 Income Balance	**65.77**	**71.24**	**85.70**	**103.44**	**118.16**	**138.50**	**152.34**	**131.34**
贷方 Credit	91.48	95.21	113.33	141.06	165.80	199.46	212.10	175.22
借方 Debit	25.71	23.97	27.63	37.62	47.65	60.96	59.76	43.88
C.经常转移差额 Current Transfers Balance	**−4.92**	**−7.51**	**−7.88**	**−7.57**	**−10.68**	**−11.51**	**−13.04**	**−12.40**
贷方 Credit	10.04	6.51	6.91	9.74	6.18	6.77	9.10	9.52
借方 Debit	14.96	14.02	14.78	17.31	16.87	18.28	22.15	21.91
二、资本和金融项目差额 Capital and Financial Account Balance	**−112.84**	**−119.23**	**−143.14**	**−149.89**	**−139.08**	**−227.79**	**−208.97**	**−162.06**
A.资本账户差额 Capital Account Balance	**−3.32**	**−4.00**	**−4.79**	**−4.88**	**−4.76**	**−4.03**	**−5.47**	**−4.99**

单位：10亿美元
Unit: USD billion

项目 Item | 年份 Year	2002	2003	2004	2005	2006	2007	2008	2009
B.金融账户差额 Financial Account Balance	**−109.51**	**−115.23**	**−138.35**	**−145.01**	**−134.32**	**−223.76**	**−203.50**	**−157.07**
1.直接投资差额 Direct Investment Balance	**−22.93**	**−22.53**	**−23.15**	**−42.22**	**−56.95**	**−51.31**	**−106.27**	**−62.79**
1.1本国对外直接投资差额 Abroad Balance	−32.02	−28.77	−30.96	−45.44	−50.17	−73.49	−130.82	−74.62
1.2外国对内直接投资差额 In Japan Balance	9.09	6.24	7.80	3.21	−6.78	22.18	24.55	11.83
2.证券投资差额 Portfolio Investment Balance	**−105.98**	**−95.11**	**22.95**	**−13.27**	**127.52**	**73.13**	**−292.60**	**−216.50**
2.1证券投资资产差额 Assets Balance	−85.93	−176.29	−173.77	−196.40	−71.04	−123.45	−189.64	−160.25
2.2证券投资负债差额 Liabilities Balance	−20.04	81.18	196.72	183.13	198.56	196.58	−102.96	−56.26
3.金融衍生工具差额 Financial Derivatives Balance	**2.48**	**5.58**	**2.41**	**−6.53**	**2.46**	**2.80**	**24.79**	**10.55**
4.其他投资差额 Other Investment Balance	**63.04**	**183.99**	**20.30**	**−60.66**	**−175.36**	**−211.86**	**201.45**	**138.59**
4.1其他投资资产差额 Other Assets Balance	36.41	149.89	−48.01	−106.60	−86.24	−260.78	139.46	202.75
4.2其他投资负债差额 Other Liabilities Balance	26.63	34.10	68.31	45.94	−89.12	48.92	61.99	−64.15
5.储备资产差额 Reserve Assets Balance	**−46.13**	**−187.15**	**−160.85**	**−22.33**	**−31.98**	**−36.52**	**−30.88**	**−26.92**
其中：外汇储备差额 Foreign Exchange Reserves Balance	−44.55	−187.33	−162.14	−25.80	−32.95	−37.06	−29.54	−6.83
三、净误差与遗漏 Net Errors and Omissions	**0.39**	**−16.99**	**−28.92**	**−15.90**	**−31.44**	**17.30**	**52.34**	**19.87**

法国国际收支概览表

Balance of Payments Abridged of France

项目 Item / 年份 Year	2002	2003	2004	2005	2006	2007	2008	2009
一、经常项目差额 Current Account Balance	**19.70**	**14.76**	**12.36**	**−9.02**	**−11.55**	**−26.62**	**−64.23**	**−59.12**
贷方 Credit	480.00	574.15	680.90	743.18	841.03	977.70	1 060.26	835.12
借方 Debit	460.30	559.39	668.54	752.20	852.58	1 004.32	1 124.48	894.24
A.货物和服务差额 Goods and Services Balance	**24.82**	**19.35**	**11.41**	**−11.32**	**−21.14**	**−35.43**	**−65.15**	**−50.24**
贷方 Credit	393.36	460.74	535.74	561.66	613.71	697.46	770.10	612.94
借方 Debit	368.54	441.40	524.32	572.99	634.85	732.89	835.25	663.18
a.货物差额 Goods Balance	**7.62**	**3.43**	**−4.85**	**−27.84**	**−38.12**	**−55.93**	**−86.88**	**−64.89**
贷方 Credit	307.20	361.93	421.11	439.45	484.77	547.42	605.22	472.26
借方 Debit	299.58	358.50	425.95	467.29	522.89	603.35	692.10	537.16
b.服务差额 Services Balance	**17.20**	**15.92**	**16.26**	**16.52**	**16.99**	**20.50**	**21.74**	**14.65**
贷方 Credit	86.16	98.81	114.63	122.21	128.94	150.05	164.89	140.67
借方 Debit	68.96	82.90	98.37	105.69	111.96	129.54	143.15	126.02
B.收益差额 Income Balance	**9.37**	**14.87**	**22.64**	**29.39**	**37.36**	**40.30**	**36.06**	**25.39**
贷方 Credit	66.87	89.36	119.72	156.12	200.21	251.43	261.06	195.43
借方 Debit	57.51	74.49	97.08	126.73	162.85	211.13	225.00	170.04
C.经常转移差额 Current Transfers Balance	**−14.49**	**−19.46**	**−21.69**	**−27.08**	**−27.77**	**−31.49**	**−35.14**	**−34.27**
贷方 Credit	19.77	24.05	25.44	25.41	27.11	28.81	29.10	26.76
借方 Debit	34.26	43.51	47.14	52.49	54.88	60.31	64.24	61.03
二、资本和金融项目差额 Capital and Financial Account Balance	**−16.54**	**3.98**	**−8.57**	**0.23**	**3.57**	**51.54**	**108.14**	**34.72**
A.资本账户差额 Capital Account Balance	**−0.21**	**−8.26**	**1.81**	**0.66**	**−0.27**	**2.47**	**1.02**	**0.44**

单位：10亿美元
Unit: USD billion

项目 Item / 年份 Year	2002	2003	2004	2005	2006	2007	2008	2009
B.金融账户差额 Financial Account Balance	**−16.32**	**12.24**	**−10.38**	**−0.43**	**3.85**	**49.07**	**107.12**	**34.29**
1.直接投资差额 Direct Investment Balance	**−1.04**	**−10.32**	**−24.10**	**−28.83**	**−39.58**	**−66.06**	**−104.43**	**−100.84**
1.1本国对外直接投资差额 Abroad Balance	−50.61	−53.38	−56.93	−113.83	−111.41	−171.97	−204.80	−162.44
1.2外国对内直接投资差额 In France Balance	49.57	43.06	32.83	85.00	71.83	105.91	100.37	61.60
2.证券投资差额 Portfolio Investment Balance	**−7.87**	**6.13**	**−66.14**	**−18.40**	**−159.08**	**−167.68**	**115.84**	**324.83**
2.1证券投资资产差额 Assets Balance	**−84.64**	**−192.71**	**−232.48**	**−243.64**	**−350.35**	**−282.14**	**−126.77**	**−92.40**
2.2证券投资负债差额 Liabilities Balance	**76.77**	**198.84**	**166.34**	**225.25**	**191.27**	**114.46**	**242.61**	**417.24**
3.金融衍生工具差额 Financial Derivatives Balance	**5.30**	**−7.05**	**6.21**	**6.36**	**4.19**	**63.08**	**−6.14**	**−1.45**
4.其他投资差额 Other Investment Balance	**−16.68**	**24.77**	**77.76**	**31.39**	**210.10**	**219.40**	**89.82**	**−178.92**
4.1其他投资资产差额 Other Assets Balance	−44.15	−14.83	−116.16	−276.85	−153.21	−264.02	64.87	82.52
4.2其他投资负债差额 Other Liabilities Balance	27.47	39.60	193.91	308.24	363.31	483.42	24.95	−261.44
5.储备资产差额 Reserve Assets Balance	**3.97**	**−1.29**	**−4.11**	**9.05**	**−11.78**	**0.33**	**12.03**	**−9.34**
其中：外汇储备差额 Foreign Exchange Reserves Balance	4.53	−1.25	−5.76	4.67	−15.41	−2.34	10.06	4.45
三、净误差与遗漏 Net Errors and Omissions	**−3.16**	**−18.74**	**−3.79**	**8.79**	**7.98**	**−24.92**	**−43.91**	**24.39**

俄罗斯国际收支概览表

Balance of Payments Abridged of Russia

项目 Item | 年份 Year	2002	2003	2004	2005	2006	2007	2008	2009
一、经常项目差额 Current Account Balance	**29.28**	**35.41**	**59.51**	**84.60**	**94.69**	**77.77**	**103.72**	**48.97**
贷方 Credit	132.48	165.75	219.27	290.73	370.81	449.48	596.00	389.64
借方 Debit	103.20	130.34	159.76	206.13	276.13	371.71	492.28	340.67
A.货物和服务差额 Goods and Services Balance	**36.93**	**48.97**	**73.13**	**104.59**	**125.66**	**112.03**	**155.43**	**91.71**
贷方 Credit	125.19	152.16	203.80	268.77	334.65	393.66	522.76	345.11
借方 Debit	88.26	103.19	130.67	164.18	209.00	281.63	367.33	253.40
a.货物差额 Goods Balance	**46.88**	**59.86**	**85.83**	**118.36**	**139.27**	**130.92**	**179.74**	**111.59**
贷方 Credit	111.20	135.93	183.21	243.80	303.55	354.40	471.60	303.39
借方 Debit	64.32	76.07	97.38	125.43	164.28	223.49	291.86	191.80
b.服务差额 Services Balance	**−9.95**	**−10.89**	**−12.69**	**−13.77**	**−13.61**	**−18.89**	**−24.31**	**−19.88**
贷方 Credit	13.99	16.23	20.59	24.97	31.10	39.26	51.16	41.72
借方 Debit	23.94	27.12	33.29	38.75	44.72	58.14	75.47	61.60
B.收益差额 Income Balance	**−6.98**	**−13.17**	**−12.77**	**−18.95**	**−29.43**	**−30.75**	**−48.94**	**−40.24**
贷方 Credit	5.80	11.06	12.00	17.48	29.76	47.40	62.27	35.77
借方 Debit	12.77	24.23	24.77	36.42	59.19	78.15	111.22	76.00
C.经常转移差额 Current Transfers Balance	**−0.67**	**−0.39**	**−0.85**	**−1.04**	**−1.54**	**−3.51**	**−2.76**	**−2.50**
贷方 Credit	1.49	2.54	3.47	4.49	6.40	8.42	10.97	8.76
借方 Debit	2.16	2.92	4.32	5.53	7.94	11.93	13.73	11.27
二、资本和金融项目差额 Capital and Financial Account Balance	**−21.69**	**−26.23**	**−53.64**	**−76.71**	**−104.20**	**−64.42**	**−92.40**	**−47.75**
A.资本账户差额 Capital Account Balance	**−16.56**	**−0.99**	**−1.62**	**−12.76**	**0.19**	**−10.22**	**0.50**	**−11.65**

单位：10亿美元
Unit: USD billion

项目 Item | 年份 Year	2002	2003	2004	2005	2006	2007	2008	2009
B.金融账户差额 Financial Account Balance	**-5.12**	**-25.24**	**-52.02**	**-63.94**	**-104.40**	**-54.20**	**-92.90**	**-36.10**
1.直接投资差额 Direct Investment Balance	**-0.59**	**-1.77**	**1.66**	**0.12**	**6.55**	**9.16**	**19.37**	**-7.33**
1.1本国对外直接投资差额 Abroad Balance	-3.97	-9.73	-13.78	-12.77	-23.15	-45.92	-56.09	-46.06
1.2外国对内直接投资差额 In Russia Balance	3.38	7.96	15.44	12.89	29.70	55.07	75.46	38.72
2.证券投资差额 Portfolio Investment Balance	**4.95**	**-4.51**	**0.62**	**-11.38**	**15.70**	**5.98**	**-35.19**	**-2.73**
2.1证券投资资产差额 Assets Balance	-1.05	-2.18	-3.82	-10.67	6.25	-9.99	-7.84	-10.90
2.2证券投资负债差额 Liabilities Balance	6.00	-2.33	4.44	-0.71	9.45	15.98	-27.35	8.17
3.金融衍生工具差额 Financial Derivatives Balance	**0.03**	**0.64**	**-0.10**	**-0.23**	**-0.10**	**0.33**	**-1.37**	**-3.24**
4.其他投资差额 Other Investment Balance	**-2.67**	**6.76**	**-8.97**	**9.01**	**-19.08**	**79.26**	**-114.62**	**-19.43**
4.1其他投资资产差额 Other Assets Balance	-4.74	-15.89	-26.64	-33.33	-49.42	-60.06	-177.49	7.46
4.2其他投资负债差额 Other Liabilities Balance	2.08	22.65	17.68	42.34	30.34	139.32	62.87	-26.89
5.储备资产差额 Reserve Assets Balance	**-6.84**	**-26.36**	**-45.24**	**-61.46**	**-107.47**	**-148.93**	**38.92**	**-3.36**
其中：外汇储备差额 Foreign Exchange Reserves Balance	-6.84	-26.37	-45.23	-61.26	-107.39	-148.86	39.58	6.35
三、净误差与遗漏 Net Errors and Omissions	**-7.59**	**-9.18**	**-5.87**	**-7.90**	**9.52**	**-13.35**	**-11.32**	**-1.22**

韩国国际收支概览表

Balance of Payments Abridged of Korea

项目 Item / 年份 Year	2002	2003	2004	2005	2006	2007	2008	2009
一、经常项目差额 Current Account Balance	**5.39**	**11.95**	**28.17**	**14.98**	**5.39**	**5.88**	**−5.78**	**42.67**
贷方 Credit	206.02	245.28	318.15	354.54	405.87	473.33	547.29	460.26
借方 Debit	200.62	233.33	289.98	339.56	400.48	467.46	553.06	417.59
A.货物和服务差额 Goods and Services Balance	**6.58**	**14.53**	**29.52**	**19.02**	**8.94**	**8.40**	**−11.00**	**38.92**
贷方 Credit	191.80	230.25	299.59	334.10	381.73	442.39	510.10	432.10
借方 Debit	185.22	215.72	270.07	315.08	372.79	433.99	521.10	393.17
a.货物差额 Goods Balance	**14.78**	**21.95**	**37.57**	**32.68**	**27.91**	**28.17**	**5.67**	**56.13**
贷方 Credit	163.41	197.29	257.71	288.97	331.84	379.05	432.92	373.58
借方 Debit	148.64	175.34	220.14	256.29	303.94	350.88	427.25	317.46
b.服务差额 Services Balance	**−8.20**	**−7.42**	**−8.05**	**−13.66**	**−18.96**	**−19.77**	**−16.67**	**−17.20**
贷方 Credit	28.39	32.96	41.88	45.13	49.89	63.35	77.18	58.51
借方 Debit	36.59	40.38	49.93	58.79	68.85	83.12	93.85	75.72
B.收益差额 Income Balance	**0.43**	**0.33**	**1.08**	**−1.56**	**0.53**	**1.00**	**5.90**	**4.55**
贷方 Credit	6.90	7.18	9.41	10.43	14.55	19.78	23.12	15.70
借方 Debit	6.47	6.85	8.33	11.99	14.01	18.78	17.22	11.15
C.经常转移差额 Current Transfers Balance	**−1.62**	**−2.90**	**−2.43**	**−2.48**	**−4.09**	**−3.53**	**−0.67**	**−0.81**
贷方 Credit	7.31	7.86	9.15	10.00	9.59	11.16	14.07	12.46
借方 Debit	8.93	10.76	11.58	12.49	13.68	14.69	14.74	13.27
二、资本和金融项目差额 Capital and Financial Account Balance	**−5.52**	**−11.88**	**−31.07**	**−15.10**	**−4.12**	**−8.00**	**6.36**	**−42.57**
A.资本账户差额 Capital Account Balance	**−1.09**	**−1.40**	**−1.75**	**−2.34**	**−3.13**	**−2.39**	**0.11**	**1.19**

单位：10亿美元
Unit: USD billion

项目 Item / 年份 Year	2002	2003	2004	2005	2006	2007	2008	2009
B.金融账户差额 Financial Account Balance	**−4.43**	**−10.48**	**−29.32**	**−12.76**	**−0.99**	**−5.61**	**6.25**	**−43.76**
1.直接投资差额 Direct Investment Balance	**−0.22**	**0.10**	**4.60**	**2.02**	**−4.54**	**−13.84**	**−15.63**	**−9.07**
1.1本国对外直接投资差额 Abroad Balance	−2.62	−3.43	−4.65	−4.29	−8.13	−15.62	−18.94	−10.57
1.2外国对内直接投资差额 In Korea Balance	2.39	3.53	9.25	6.31	3.59	1.78	3.31	1.51
2.证券投资差额 Portfolio Investment Balance	**0.35**	**18.30**	**8.46**	**−0.02**	**−19.95**	**−26.06**	**−2.41**	**50.68**
2.1证券投资资产差额 Assets Balance	−5.03	−4.39	−9.92	−14.14	−28.01	−56.44	23.48	1.30
2.2证券投资负债差额 Liabilities Balance	5.38	22.69	18.37	14.11	8.06	30.38	−25.89	49.38
3.金融衍生工具差额 Financial Derivatives Balance	**0.36**	**−0.39**	**0.16**	**−1.71**	**−2.80**	**5.44**	**−14.77**	**−5.54**
4.其他投资差额 Other Investment Balance	**6.85**	**−2.70**	**−3.86**	**6.81**	**48.38**	**43.96**	**−17.38**	**−10.77**
4.1其他投资资产差额 Other Assets Balance	1.59	−5.13	−8.14	−2.66	−7.95	−16.76	−13.74	0.38
4.2其他投资负债差额 Other Liabilities Balance	5.26	2.43	4.28	9.47	56.33	60.73	−3.64	−11.16
5.储备资产差额 Reserve Assets Balance	**−11.77**	**−25.79**	**−38.68**	**−19.86**	**−22.09**	**−15.13**	**56.45**	**−69.06**
其中：外汇储备差额 Foreign Exchange Reserves Balance	−11.53	−25.61	−38.66	−20.27	−21.97	−15.26	56.74	−65.03
三、净误差与遗漏 Net Errors and Omissions	**0.12**	**−0.07**	**2.90**	**0.12**	**−1.27**	**2.12**	**−0.59**	**−0.10**

中国国际投资头寸表

China's International Investment Position

项目 Item	2004年末 End-2004	2005年末 End-2005	2006年末 End-2006	2007年末 End-2007	2008年末 End-2008	2009年末 End-2009
净头寸Net	**2 764**	**4 077**	**6 402**	**11 881**	**14 938**	**18 219**
A.资产Assets	**9 291**	**12 233**	**16 905**	**24 162**	**29 567**	**34 601**
1.在国外直接投资Direct Investment Abroad	**527**	**645**	**906**	**1 160**	**1 857**	**2 296**
2.证券投资Portfolio Investment	**920**	**1 167**	**2 652**	**2 846**	**2 525**	**2 428**
2.1股本证券Equity Securities	0	0	15	196	214	546
2.2债务证券Debt Securities	920	1 167	2 637	2 650	2 311	1 882
3.其他投资Other Investment	**1 658**	**2 164**	**2 539**	**4 683**	**5 523**	**5 365**
3.1贸易信贷Trade Credits	432	661	922	1 160	1 102	1 646
3.2贷款Loans	590	719	670	888	1 071	942
3.3货币和存款Currency and Deposits	553	675	736	1 380	1 529	1 409
3.4其他资产Other Assets	83	109	210	1 255	1 821	1 368
4.储备资产Reserve Assets	**6 186**	**8 257**	**10 808**	**15 473**	**19 662**	**24 513**
4.1货币黄金Monetary Gold	41	42	123	170	169	371
4.2特别提款权Special Drawing Right	12	12	11	12	12	125
4.3在基金组织中的储备头寸Reserve Position in the Fund	33	14	11	8	20	25
4.4外汇Foreign Exchange	6 099	8 189	10 663	15 282	19 460	23 992

单位：亿美元
Unit: USD 100 million

项目 Item	2004年末 End-2004	2005年末 End-2005	2006年末 End-2006	2007年末 End-2007	2008年末 End-2008	2009年末 End-2009
B. 负债Liabilities	**6 527**	**8 156**	**10 503**	**12 281**	**14 629**	**16 381**
1. 外国来华直接投资 Direct Investment in Reporting Economy	**3 690**	**4 715**	**6 144**	**7 037**	**9 155**	**9 974**
2. 证券投资 Portfolio Investment	**566**	**766**	**1 207**	**1 466**	**1 677**	**1 900**
2.1股本证券Equity Securities	433	636	1 065	1 290	1 505	1 748
2.2债务证券Debt Securities	133	130	142	176	172	152
3. 其他投资 Other Investment	**2 271**	**2 675**	**3 152**	**3 778**	**3 796**	**4 508**
3.1贸易信贷Trade Credits	809	1 063	1 196	1 487	1 296	1 617
3.2贷款Loans	880	870	985	1 033	1 030	1 114
3.3货币和存款Currency and Deposits	381	484	595	791	918	1 034
3.4其他负债Other Liabilities	200	257	377	467	552	742

外汇储备

Foreign Exchange Reserves

单位：亿美元
Unit: USD 100 million

年份 Year	外汇储备余额 Foreign Exchange Reserves	外汇储备增加额 Increase of Foreign Exchange Reserves
1990	111	55
1991	217	106
1992	194	−23
1993	212	18
1994	516	304
1995	736	220
1996	1 050	315
1997	1 399	348
1998	1 450	51
1999	1 547	97
2000	1 656	109
2001	2 122	466
2002	2 864	742
2003	4 033	1 168
2004	6 099	2 067
2005	8 189	2 090
2006	10 663	2 475
2007	15 282	4 619
2008	19 460	4 178
2009	23 992	4 531

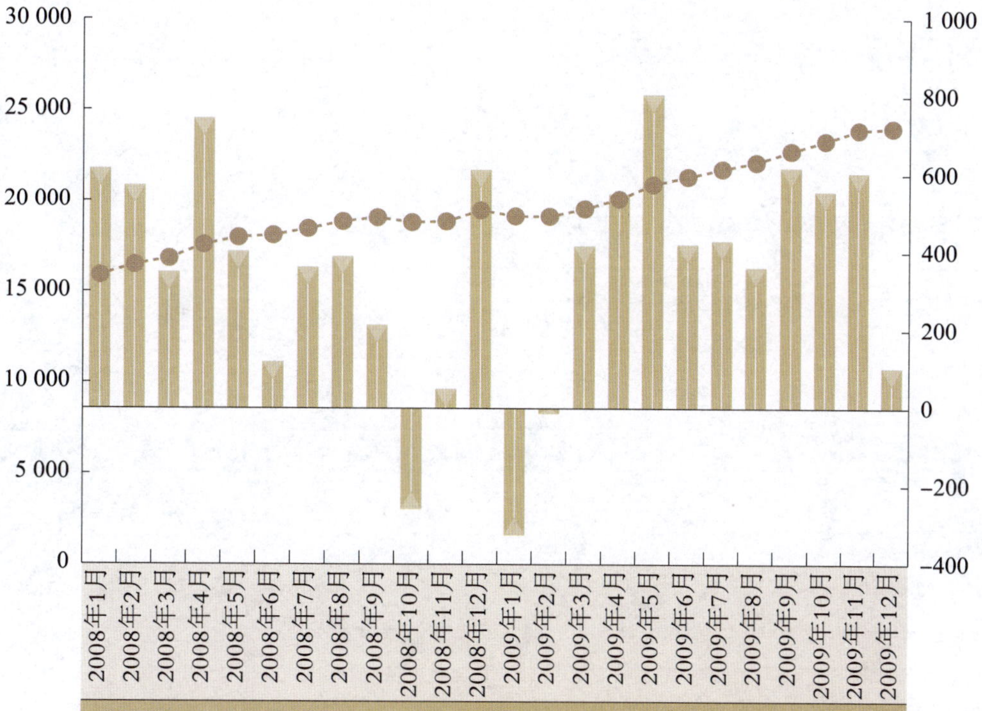

月度外汇储备余额及其变动情况 ● Change of Monthly Foreign Exchange Reserves

外汇储备增加额（右坐标）Increase of Foreign Exchange Reserves (RHS)

外汇储备余额（左坐标）Foreign Exchange Reserves (LHS)

亿美元
USD 100 million

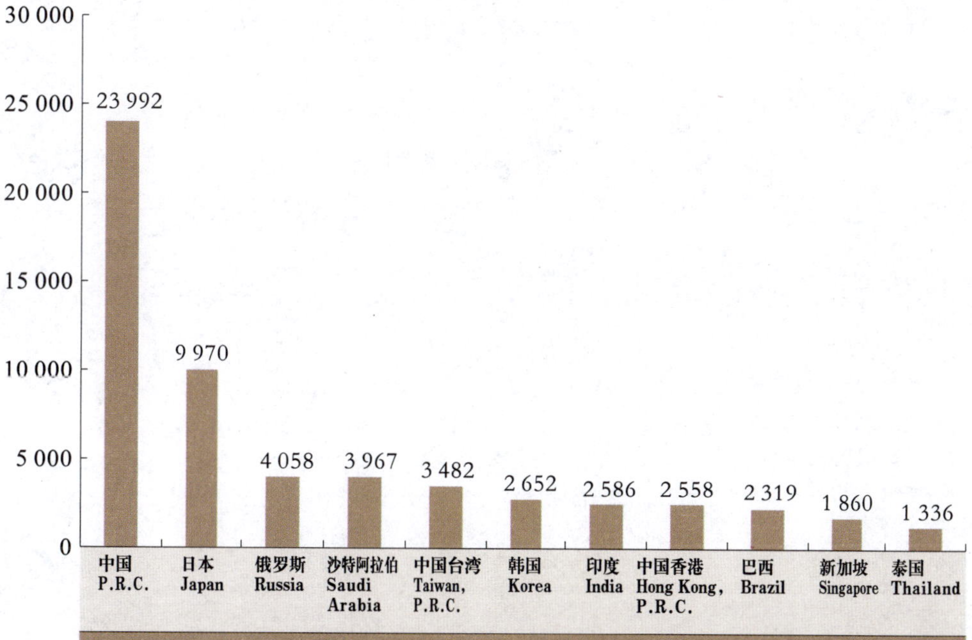

2009年末部分国家和地区外汇储备 ● Foreign Reserves of Some Countries/Regions, End of 2009

亿美元
USD 100 million

二、对外贸易①

Ⅱ. Foreign Trade

2009年世界货物贸易出口前十名

Top 10 Countries/Regions of Goods Export in 2009

国家/地区 Countries/Regions	出口额（10亿美元） Export（USD billion）	增长 Increase（%）	占世界出口总额比重 Ratio to total Export of the World（%）	2008年排名 Ranking in 2008
世界World	12 461	−23	100.0	
1.中国P.R.C.	1 202	−16	9.6	2
2.德国Germany	1 121	−22	9.0	1
3.美国U.S.A	1 057	−18	8.5	3
4.日本Japan	581	−26	4.7	4
5.荷兰Netherlands	499	−22	4.0	5
6.法国France	475	−21	3.8	6
7.意大利Italy	405	−25	3.2	7
8.比利时Belgium	370	−22	3.0	8
9.韩国Korea	364	−14	2.9	12
10.英国U.K.	351	−24	2.8	10

① 数据来源：海关总署；世界贸易组织。
Sources：General Administration of Customs；World Trade Organization.

2009年世界货物贸易进口前十名

Top 10 Countries/Regions of Goods Import in 2009

国家/地区 Countries/Regions	进口额（10亿美元） Import（USD billion）	增长 Increase（%）	占世界进口总额比重 Ratio to total Import of the World（%）	2008年排名 Ranking in 2008
世界World	12 647	−23	100.0	
1.美国U.S.A	1 604	−26	12.7	1
2.中国P.R.C.	1 006	−11	8.0	3
3.德国Germany	931	−21	7.4	2
4.法国France	551	−22	4.4	5
5.日本Japan	551	−28	4.4	4
6.英国U.K.	480	−24	3.8	6
7.荷兰Netherlands	446	−23	3.5	7
8.意大利Italy	410	−26	3.2	8
9.中国香港Hong Kong,P.R.C.	353	−10	2.8	13
10.比利时Belgium	351	−25	2.8	9

中国进出口总值

单位：亿美元
Unit: USD 100 million

China's Total Value of Import & Export

年度 Year	进出口 Import & Export	出口 Export	进口 Import	差额 Balance
1981	440	220	220	0
1982	416	223	193	30
1983	436	222	214	8
1984	535	261	274	−13
1985	696	274	423	−149
1986	738	309	429	−120
1987	827	394	432	−38
1988	1 028	475	553	−78
1989	1 117	525	591	−66
1990	1 154	621	534	87
1991	1 357	719	638	81
1992	1 655	849	806	44
1993	1 957	917	1 040	−122
1994	2 366	1 210	1 156	54
1995	2 809	1 488	1 321	167
1996	2 899	1 511	1 388	122
1997	3 252	1 828	1 424	404
1998	3 239	1 837	1 402	435
1999	3 606	1 949	1 657	292
2000	4 743	2 492	2 251	241
2001	5 097	2 661	2 436	226
2002	6 208	3 256	2 952	304
2003	8 510	4 382	4 128	255
2004	11 546	5 933	5 612	321
2005	14 219	7 620	6 600	1 020
2006	17 604	9 689	7 915	1 775
2007	21 766	12 205	9 561	2 643
2008	25 633	14 307	11 326	2 981
2009	22 072	12 017	10 056	1 961

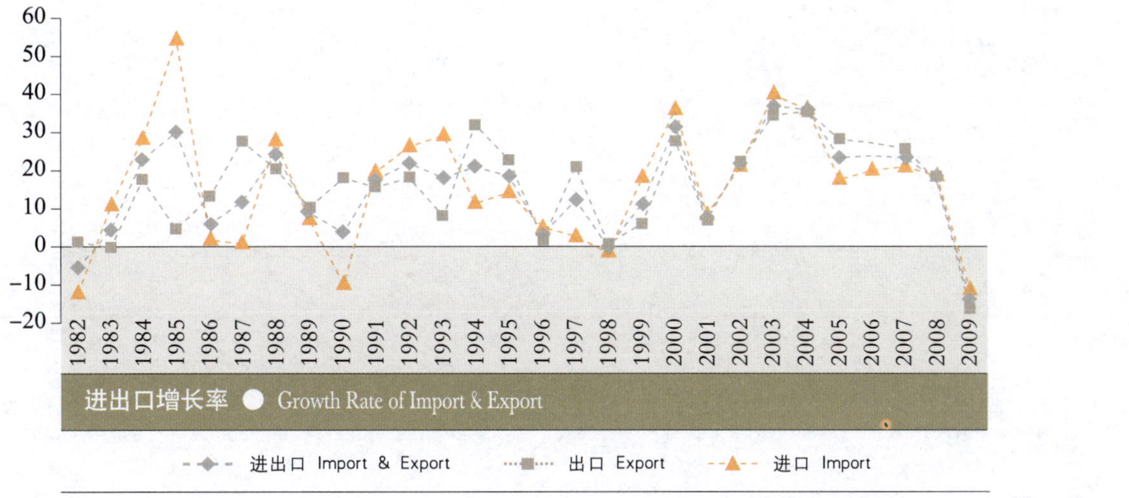

进出口增长率 ● Growth Rate of Import & Export

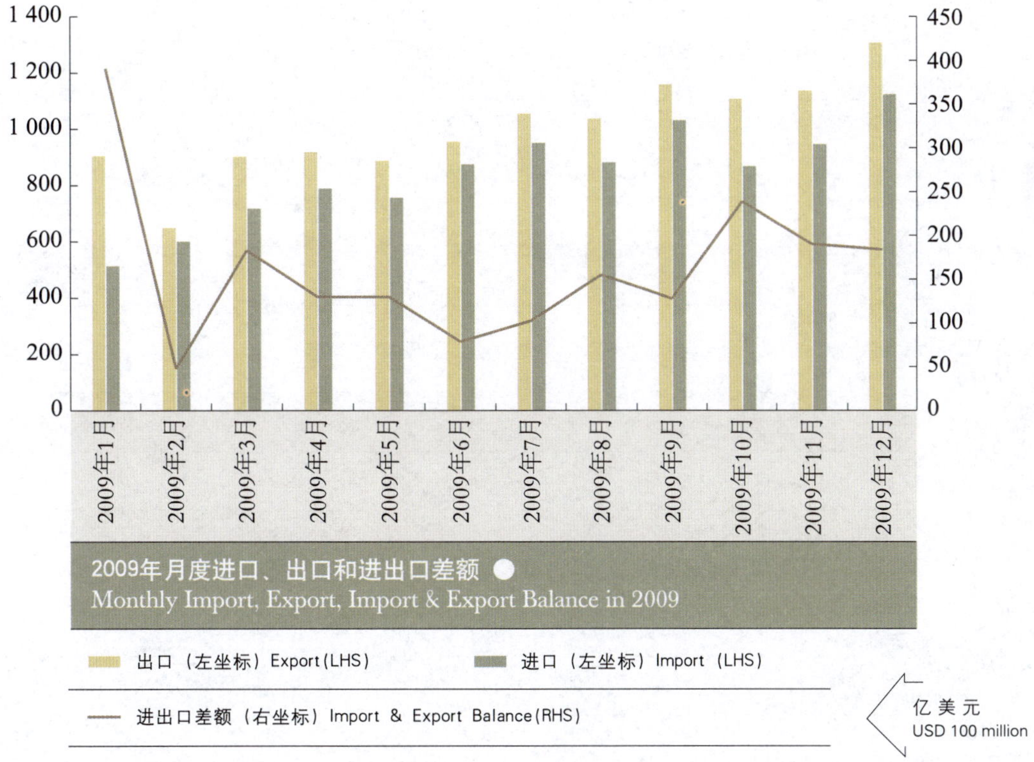

2009年月度进口、出口和进出口差额 ●
Monthly Import, Export, Import & Export Balance in 2009

按贸易方式分类进出口

Import & Export by Trading Forms

贸易方式 Trading Forms	2001	2002	2003	2004	2005	2006	2007	2008	2009
进口 Import	**243 613**	**295 203**	**412 836**	**561 423**	**660 118**	**791 614**	**955 818**	**1 133 086**	**1 005 555**
一般贸易 Ordinary Trade	113 470	129 122	187 700	248 227	279 719	333 181	428 648	572 677	533 872
国家间、国际组织间无偿援助和捐赠的物资 Foreign Aid and Donation by Overseas	138	86	114	98	49	65	35	49	43
其他捐赠物资 Other Donations	13	13	21	12	19	22	10	58	136
来料加工装配贸易 Processing and Assembling Trade	28 863	34 184	39 125	53 721	67 029	73 834	89 165	90 162	75 993
进料加工贸易 Processing with Imported Materials	65 120	88 032	123 810	168 020	206 997	247 662	279 228	288 243	246 345
寄售代销贸易 Goods on Consignment	7	8	6	8	6	3	2	2	2
边境小额贸易 Border Trade	3 284	3 870	4 303	5 043	5 721	6 214	7 589	8 975	7 196
加工贸易进口设备 Equipment Imported for Processing & Assembling	1 616	1 727	1 961	2 603	2 862	2 817	3 277	2 859	953
租赁贸易 Goods on Lease	1 825	1 407	1 392	2 223	3 681	8 067	8 280	6 932	3 448
外商投资企业作为投资进口的设备物品 Equipment or Materials Imported as Investment by Foreign-funded Enterprises	14 515	17 144	20 968	31 203	27 674	27 823	25 906	27 677	15 176
出料加工贸易 Outward Processing Trade	19	24	23	24	33	33	39	160	78
易货贸易 Barter Trade	13	8	6	13	3	6	4	1	8
免税外汇商品 Duty Free Commodities on Payment of Foreign Exchange	52	18	7	6	8	6	6	6	5
保税仓库进出境货物 Customs Warehousing Trade	5 248	5 178	7 185	11 081	20 065	32 018	41 720	57 277	54 392
保税仓储转口货物 Entrepot Trade by Bonded Area	8 341	13 430	25 147	37 720	44 255	55 508	66 910	73 739	64 259
出口加工区进口设备 Equipment Imported into Export Processing Zone	149	373	558	882	1 411	3 623	4 108	3 118	2 113
其他 Others	940	578	510	539	586	732	890	1 150	1 535

单位：百万美元
Unit: USD million

贸易方式 Trading Forms	2001	2002	2003	2004	2005	2006	2007	2008	2009
出口 Export	**266 154**	**325 565**	**438 371**	**593 368**	**761 999**	**969 073**	**1 218 015**	**1 428 546**	**1 201 663**
一般贸易 Ordinary Trade	111 916	136 204	182 034	243 635	315 091	416 318	538 576	662 584	529 833
国家间、国际组织间无偿援助和捐赠的物资 Foreign Aid and Donation by Overseas	205	160	106	187	225	211	201	231	291
其他捐赠物资 Other Donations	0	0	0	0	0	0	0	2	8
补偿贸易 Compensation Trade	18	69	17	9	0	1	0	0	0
来料加工装配贸易 Processing and Assembling Trade	42 233	47 476	54 332	68 569	83 970	94 483	116 043	110 520	93 423
进料加工贸易 Processing with Imported Materials	105 221	132 461	187 517	259 419	332 511	415 892	501 613	564 663	493 558
寄售代销贸易 Goods on Consignment	1	1	1	1	1	2	4	4	6
边境小额贸易 Border Trade	841	1 826	3 476	4 431	7 409	9 943	13 739	21 904	13 667
对外承包工程出口货物 Contracting Projects	481	551	640	1 130	1 705	3 071	5 188	10 963	13 357
租赁贸易 Goods on Lease	9	6	8	15	90	214	84	189	117
出料加工贸易 Outward Processing Trade	24	22	20	27	27	24	44	118	46
易货贸易 Barter Trade	56	74	41	28	17	19	48	16	1
保税仓库进出境货物 Customs Warehousing Trade	2 759	3 134	4 017	5 739	7 956	13 069	18 624	28 404	26 793
保税仓储转口货物 Entrepot Trade by Bonded Area	1 663	3 253	5 488	9 354	11 615	14 463	20 977	23 937	21 476
其他 Others	727	329	674	824	1 380	1 361	2 916	5 011	9 088

按企业类型分类进出口

Import & Export by Type of Enterprises

单位：亿美元
Unit: USD 100 million

企业类型Type of Enterprises	2001	2002	2003	2004	2005	2006	2007	2008	2009
进口Import	**2 436**	**2 952**	**4 128**	**5 614**	**6 601**	**7 916**	**9 558**	**11 331**	**10 056**
国有企业 State-owned Enterprises	1 035	1 145	1 425	1 765	1 972	2 252	2 697	3 538	2 885
外商投资企业 Foreign-funded Enterprises	1 259	1 603	2 319	3 246	3 875	4 726	5 594	6 200	5 452
中外合作 Sino-foreign Contractual Joint Ventures	77	84	100	107	96	99	88	88	66
中外合资 Sino-foreign Equity Joint Ventures	564	608	809	1 092	1 184	1 356	1 549	1 818	1 586
外商独资 Foreign Investment Enterprises	618	911	1 411	2 046	2 595	3 270	3 957	4 294	3 799
集体企业 Collective Enterprises	80	95	132	177	205	200	232	289	265
其他 Other Enterprises	62	110	252	427	549	738	1 035	1 304	1 454
出口Export	**2 662**	**3 256**	**4 384**	**5 934**	**7 620**	**9 691**	**12 180**	**14 285**	**12 017**
国有企业 State-owned Enterprises	1 132	1 229	1 380	1 536	1 688	1 913	2 248	2 572	1 910
外商投资企业 Foreign-funded Enterprises	1 332	1 699	2 403	3 386	4 442	5 638	6 955	7 906	6 722
中外合作 Sino-foreign Contractual Joint Ventures	102	117	132	148	157	177	181	183	146
中外合资 Sino-foreign Equity Joint Ventures	541	621	810	1 096	1 360	1 638	1 988	2 269	1 824
外商独资 Foreign Investment Enterprises	690	962	1 461	2 142	2 925	3 824	4 786	5 454	4 752
集体企业 Collective Enterprises	142	189	251	318	365	411	469	547	405
其他 Other Enterprises	55	139	349	694	1 125	1 728	2 508	3 260	2 979
差额Balance	**225**	**304**	**255**	**319**	**1 019**	**1 775**	**2 622**	**2 955**	**1 961**
国有企业 State-owned Enterprises	97	84	−44	−229	−284	−339	−449	−966	−975
外商投资企业 Foreign-funded Enterprises	74	97	84	140	567	912	1 361	1 706	1 270
中外合作 Sino-foreign Contractual Joint Ventures	24	33	33	40	61	78	93	95	80
中外合资 Sino-foreign Equity Joint Ventures	−23	13	2	4	176	281	439	451	238
外商独资 Foreign Investment Enterprises	72	51	50	96	330	553	829	1 160	953
集体企业 Collective Enterprises	62	94	119	141	160	211	237	258	140
其他 Other Enterprises	−7	29	97	267	576	990	1 473	1 956	1 525

2009年按贸易方式分类的进口构成
Components of Import by Trading Forms in 2009

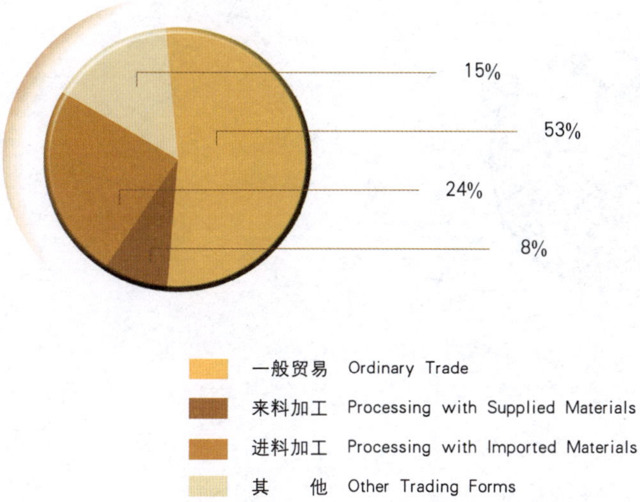

2009年按贸易方式分类的出口构成
Components of Export by Trading Forms in 2009

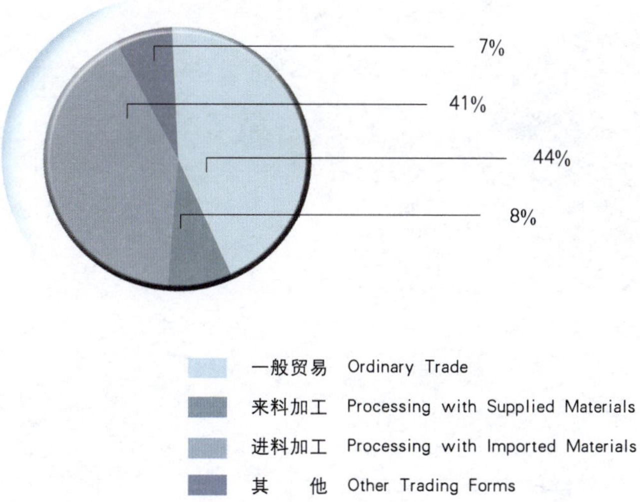

2009年按企业类型分类的进口构成
Components of Import by Type of Enterprises in 2009

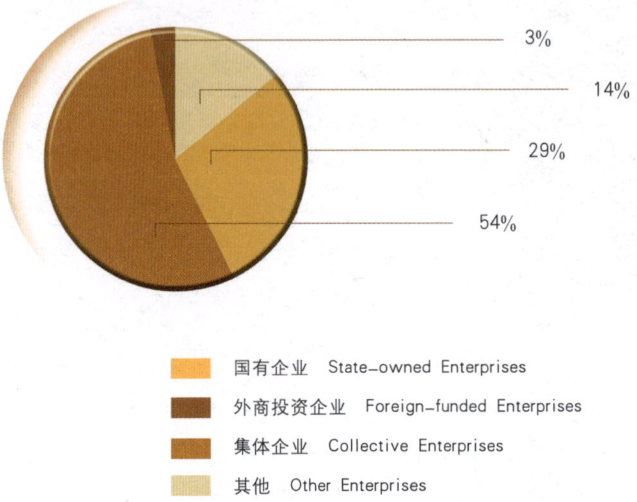

2009年按企业类型分类的出口构成
Components of Export by Type of Enterprises in 2009

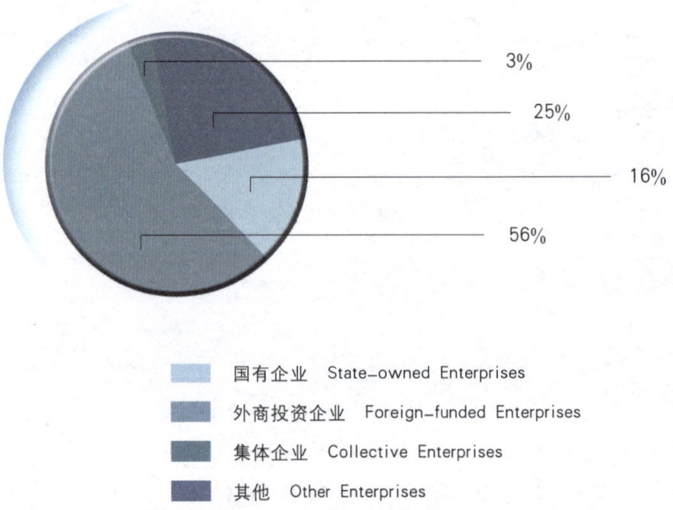

2009年进出口按贸易方式分类

单位：亿美元
Unit: USD 100 million

Import & Export by Trading Forms in 2009

贸易方式 Trading Forms	进口 Import 金额Value	进口 Import 同比(%)Increase	出口 Export 金额Value	出口 Export 同比(%)Increase	进出口差额 Import & Export Balance
总值 Total Value	**10 056**	**−11.2**	**12 017**	**−16.0**	**1 961**
一般贸易 Ordinary Trade	5 339	−6.7	5 298	−20.1	41
加工贸易 Processing Trade	3 223	−14.8	5 870	−13.1	2 647
来料加工 With Supplied Material	760	−15.7	934	−15.5	174
进料加工 With Imported Material	2 463	−14.5	4 936	−12.6	2 473
其他贸易 Other Trading Forms	1 494	−17.9	849	−6.5	−645

2009年进出口按企业类型分类

Import & Export by Type of Enterprises in 2009

单位：亿美元
Unit: USD 100 million

企业类型 Type of Enterprises	进口 Import 金额Value	进口 Import 同比(%)Increase	出口 Export 金额Value	出口 Export 同比(%)Increase	进出口差额 Import & Export Balance
总值 Total Value	**10 056**	**-11.2**	**12 017**	**-16.0**	**1 961**
国有企业 State-owned Enterprises	2 885	-18.5	1 910	-25.8	-975
外资企业 Foreign-funded Enterprises	5 452	-12.0	6 722	-15.0	1 270
集体企业 Collective Enterprises	265	-8.2	405	-25.9	140
其他企业 Other Enterprises	1 454	11.4	2 979	-9.2	1 525

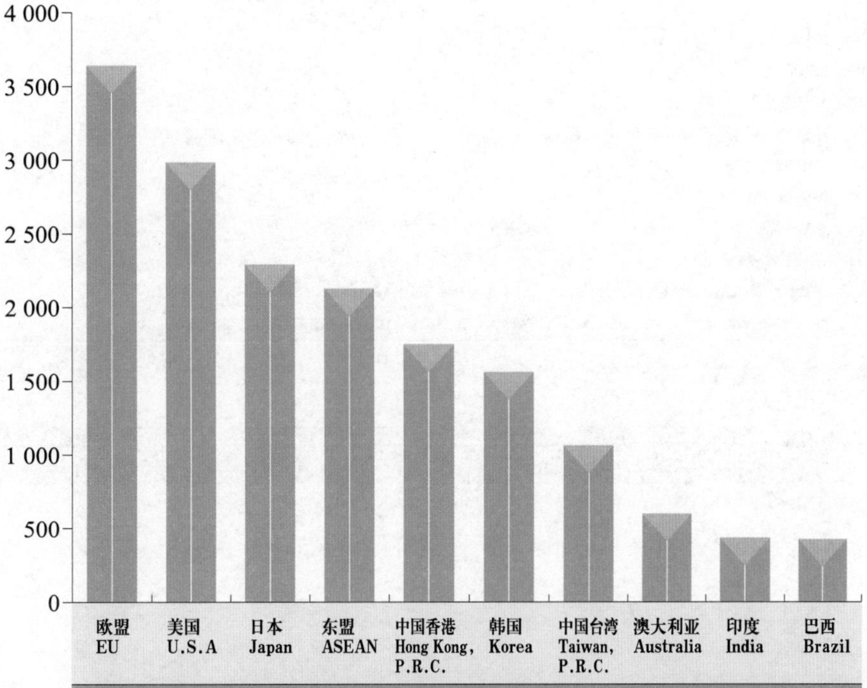

2009年前十位贸易伙伴（按进出口总值）

Top 10 Trading Partners in 2009 (Based on the Total Value of Import & Export)

亿美元

USD 100 million

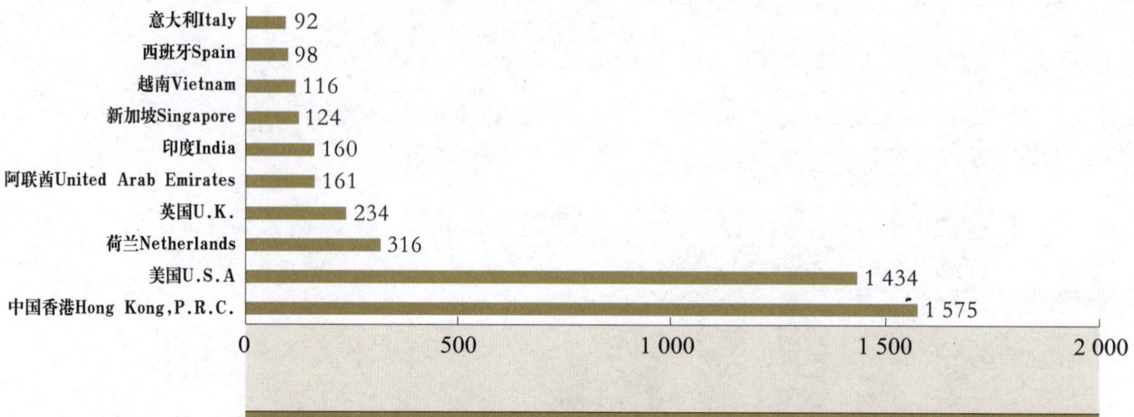

2009年前十位贸易顺差来源地 ● Top 10 Sources of Trade Surplus in 2009

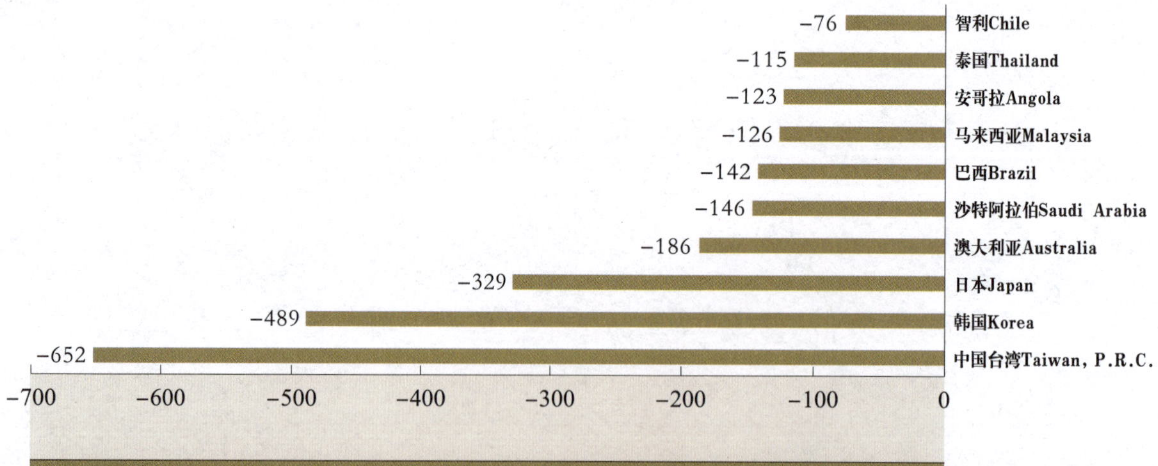

2009年前十位贸易逆差来源地 ● Top 10 Sources of Trade Deficit in 2009

三、外汇市场和人民币汇率①

Ⅲ. Foreign Exchange Market and Exchange Rate of RMB

人民币对美元交易中间价月平均汇价

人民币元/100美元
RMB per 100 USD

Monthly Average Transaction Mid Rates of RMB against USD, 1980–2009

月份 Month	1980年	1981年	1982年	1983年	1984年	1985年	1986年	1987年	1988年	1989年
1月/Jan.	149.37	154.87	176.77	192.01	204.12	280.88	320.15	372.21	372.21	372.21
2月/Feb.	150.05	161.06	181.74	196.03	205.72	282.51	320.70	372.21	372.21	372.21
3月/Mar.	155.12	162.80	183.79	197.80	206.08	284.51	321.20	372.21	372.21	372.21
4月/Apr.	155.70	166.20	185.19	198.72	208.91	284.11	320.61	372.21	372.21	372.21
5月/May	149.06	172.27	180.97	198.52	218.21	284.75	319.44	372.21	372.21	372.21
6月/Jun.	146.50	176.05	189.70	198.95	221.22	286.25	320.35	372.21	372.21	372.21
7月/Jul.	145.25	175.98	192.36	198.88	229.39	287.38	363.82	372.21	372.21	372.21
8月/Aug.	147.26	179.52	193.87	198.00	236.43	290.23	370.36	372.21	372.21	372.21
9月/Sep.	146.81	175.01	195.04	198.14	253.26	296.26	370.66	372.21	372.21	372.21
10月/Oct.	148.03	175.05	198.22	196.17	264.00	306.73	371.64	372.21	372.21	372.21
11月/Nov.	151.73	173.46	199.41	198.90	266.16	320.15	372.21	372.21	372.21	372.21
12月/Dec.	154.19	173.78	193.99	198.69	278.91	320.15	372.21	372.21	372.21	423.82
年平均 Annual Average	**149.84**	**170.50**	**189.25**	**197.57**	**232.70**	**293.66**	**345.28**	**372.21**	**372.21**	**376.51**

①资料来源：国家外汇管理局。
Sources: State Administration of Foreign Exchange.

人民币对美元交易中间价月平均汇价

Monthly Average Transaction Mid Rates of RMB Against USD, 1980–2009

月份 Month	1990年	1991年	1992年	1993年	1994年	1995年	1996年	1997年	1998年	1999年
1月/Jan.	472.21	522.21	544.81	576.40	870.00	844.13	831.86	829.63	827.91	827.90
2月/Feb.	472.21	522.21	546.35	576.99	870.28	843.54	831.32	829.29	827.91	827.80
3月/Mar.	472.21	522.21	547.34	573.13	870.23	842.76	832.89	829.57	827.92	827.91
4月/Apr.	472.21	526.59	549.65	570.63	869.55	842.25	833.15	829.57	827.92	827.92
5月/May	472.21	531.39	550.36	572.17	866.49	831.28	832.88	829.29	827.90	827.85
6月/Jun.	472.21	535.35	547.51	573.74	865.72	830.08	832.26	829.21	827.97	827.80
7月/Jul.	472.21	535.55	544.32	576.12	864.03	830.07	831.60	829.11	827.98	827.77
8月/Aug.	472.21	537.35	542.87	577.64	858.98	830.75	830.81	828.94	827.99	827.73
9月/Sep.	472.21	537.35	549.48	578.70	854.03	831.88	830.44	828.72	827.89	827.74
10月/Oct.	472.21	537.90	553.69	578.68	852.93	831.55	830.00	828.38	827.78	827.74
11月/Nov.	495.54	538.58	561.31	579.47	851.69	831.35	829.93	828.11	827.78	827.82
12月/Dec.	522.21	541.31	579.82	580.68	848.45	831.56	829.90	827.96	827.79	827.93
年平均 Annual Average	**478.32**	**532.33**	**551.46**	**576.20**	**861.87**	**835.10**	**831.42**	**828.98**	**827.91**	**827.83**

人民币元/100美元
RMB per 100 USD

月份 Month	2000年	2001年	2002年	2003年	2004年	2005年	2006年	2007年	2008年	2009年
1 月/Jan.	827.93	827.71	827.67	827.68	827.69	827.65	806.68	778.98	724.78	683.82
2 月/Feb.	827.79	827.70	827.66	827.73	827.71	827.65	804.93	775.46	716.01	683.57
3 月/Mar.	827.86	827.76	827.70	827.72	827.71	827.65	803.50	773.90	707.52	683.41
4 月/Apr.	827.93	827.71	827.72	827.71	827.69	827.65	801.56	772.47	700.07	683.12
5 月/May	827.77	827.72	827.69	827.69	827.71	827.65	801.52	767.04	697.24	682.45
6 月/Jun.	827.72	827.71	827.70	827.71	827.67	827.65	800.67	763.30	689.71	683.32
7 月/Jul.	827.93	827.69	827.68	827.73	827.67	822.90	799.10	758.05	683.76	683.20
8 月/Aug.	827.96	827.70	827.67	827.70	827.68	810.19	797.33	757.53	685.15	683.22
9 月/Sep.	827.86	827.68	827.70	827.71	827.67	809.22	793.68	752.58	683.07	682.89
10 月/Oct.	827.85	827.68	827.69	827.67	827.65	808.89	790.32	750.12	683.16	682.75
11月/Nov.	827.74	827.69	827.71	827.69	827.65	808.40	786.52	742.33	682.86	682.74
12月/Dec.	827.72	827.68	827.72	827.70	827.65	807.59	782.38	736.76	684.24	682.79
年平均 Annual Average	**827.84**	**827.70**	**827.70**	**827.70**	**827.68**	**819.42**	**797.18**	**760.40**	**694.51**	**683.10**

2009年人民币交易中间价

Transaction Mid Rates of RMB in 2009

月份 Month	币种 Currency	期初价 Beginning of Period	期末价 End of Period	最高价 Highest	最低价 Lowest	期平均 Period Average	累计平均 Accumulative Average
1月 Jan.	美元 USD	683.67	683.80	683.99	683.60	683.82	683.82
	港元 HKD	88.205	88.127	88.205	88.098	88.158	88.158
	日元 JPY	7.4284	7.6715	7.6936	7.2758	7.5414	7.5414
	欧元 EUR	953.82	887.95	953.82	881.42	910.43	910.43
	英镑 GBP	991.94	946.58	1 038.09	946.58	996.88	996.88
2月 Feb.	美元 USD	683.97	683.79	683.98	683.27	683.57	683.67
	港元 HKD	88.197	88.182	88.205	88.133	88.160	88.159
	日元 JPY	7.6179	6.9924	7.6516	6.9924	7.4097	7.4661
	欧元 EUR	872.61	868.04	886.68	859.67	874.32	889.80
	英镑 GBP	986.11	975.26	1 014.22	972.97	984.47	989.79
3月 Mar.	美元 USD	683.89	683.59	683.95	682.93	683.41	683.57
	港元 HKD	88.161	88.203	88.203	88.102	88.140	88.152
	日元 JPY	7.0424	6.9630	7.2149	6.8843	6.9873	7.2813
	欧元 EUR	859.96	903.23	933.74	853.09	891.50	890.46
	英镑 GBP	972.73	977.29	1 003.57	942.27	970.64	982.40
4月 Apr.	美元 USD	683.49	682.50	683.70	682.50	683.12	683.45
	港元 HKD	88.184	88.061	88.211	88.061	88.140	88.149
	日元 JPY	6.9095	6.9803	7.0721	6.7926	6.9072	7.1806
	欧元 EUR	901.59	908.37	918.73	882.79	899.57	892.91
	英镑 GBP	977.22	1 010.27	1 027.49	977.22	1 002.64	987.85
5月 May	美元 USD	682.25	683.24	683.24	682.01	682.45	683.26
	港元 HKD	88.030	88.130	88.130	88.000	88.046	88.129
	日元 JPY	6.8668	7.1822	7.2525	6.8668	7.0681	7.1595
	欧元 EUR	908.69	955.00	956.40	906.61	929.22	899.72
	英镑 GBP	1 020.37	1 090.25	1 090.25	1 020.37	1 048.06	999.14
6月 Jun.	美元 USD	683.17	683.19	683.68	683.02	683.32	683.27
	港元 HKD	88.135	88.153	88.209	88.111	88.160	88.135
	日元 JPY	7.1913	7.1117	7.1913	6.9304	7.0765	7.1440
	欧元 EUR	963.75	964.08	976.21	941.36	957.89	910.56
	英镑 GBP	1 105.10	1 133.79	1 133.79	1 091.65	1 117.82	1 021.27
7月 Jul.	美元 USD	683.25	683.23	683.36	683.07	683.20	683.26
	港元 HKD	88.160	88.158	88.174	88.138	88.153	88.138
	日元 JPY	7.0895	7.1580	7.3625	7.0761	7.2311	7.1582
	欧元 EUR	959.11	962.50	972.29	948.78	961.45	918.86
	英镑 GBP	1 125.35	1 127.81	1 128.36	1 098.23	1 118.16	1 037.07

人民币元/100外币
RMB per 100 Foreign Currency

月份 Month	币种 Currency	期初价 Beginning of Period	期末价 End of Period	最高价 Highest	最低价 Lowest	期平均 Period Average	累计平均 Accumulative Average
8月 Aug.	美元 USD	683.10	683.12	683.52	683.03	683.22	683.26
	港元 HKD	88.141	88.133	88.193	88.128	88.150	88.140
	日元 JPY	7.2087	7.3537	7.3537	7.0347	7.1994	7.1636
	欧元 EUR	974.10	977.27	984.33	964.43	974.67	926.10
	英镑 GBP	1 143.24	1 112.94	1 160.72	1 108.42	1 131.05	1 049.25
9月 Sep.	美元 USD	683.08	682.90	683.16	682.71	682.89	683.21
	港元 HKD	88.130	88.114	88.138	88.087	88.110	88.136
	日元 JPY	7.3390	7.5747	7.6744	7.3390	7.4638	7.1995
	欧元 EUR	978.85	996.59	1 009.59	970.33	993.54	934.16
	英镑 GBP	1 111.47	1 090.90	1 137.17	1 080.21	1 114.15	1 057.01
10月 Oct.	美元 USD	682.70	682.81	682.85	682.67	682.75	683.18
	港元 HKD	88.089	88.102	88.109	88.086	88.096	88.133
	日元 JPY	7.6937	7.4763	7.6937	7.4117	7.5275	7.2257
	欧元 EUR	1 008.07	1 012.88	1 026.92	1 003.62	1 015.61	940.68
	英镑 GBP	1 094.85	1 129.85	1 136.78	1 079.83	1 110.19	1 061.27
11月 Nov.	美元 USD	682.82	682.72	682.82	682.67	682.74	683.13
	港元 HKD	88.104	88.091	88.104	88.086	88.094	88.129
	日元 JPY	7.5797	7.8800	7.9447	7.5260	7.6512	7.2661
	欧元 EUR	1 006.24	1 023.50	1 032.38	1 005.05	1 018.60	948.08
	英镑 GBP	1 123.00	1 127.00	1 149.14	1 119.64	1 134.08	1 068.19
12月 Dec.	美元 USD	682.70	682.82	682.87	682.68	682.79	683.10
	港元 HKD	88.089	88.048	88.098	88.030	88.069	88.123
	日元 JPY	7.9002	7.3782	7.9002	7.3782	7.6101	7.2986
	欧元 EUR	1 025.18	979.71	1 030.47	973.19	997.08	952.70
	英镑 GBP	1 122.80	1 097.80	1 137.17	1 085.02	1 108.36	1 071.97

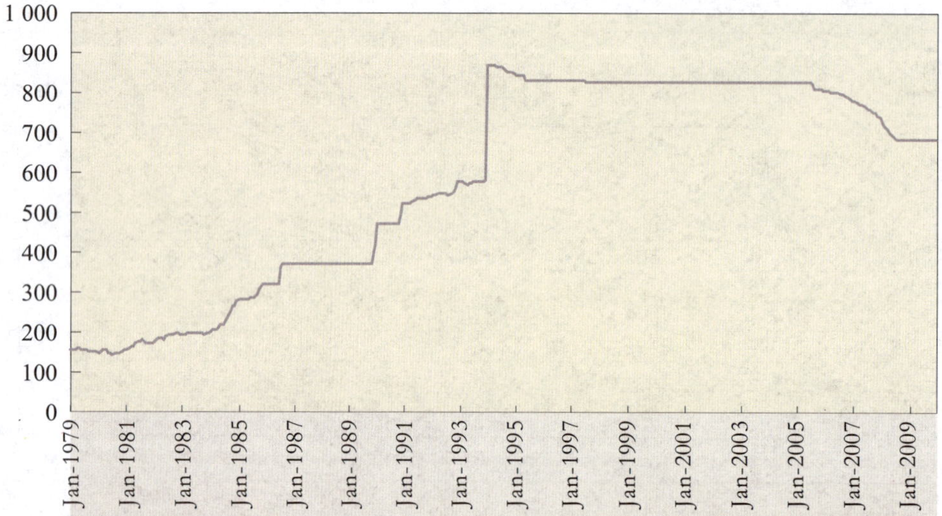

1979—2009年人民币对美元交易中间价月平均汇价
Monthly Average Transaction Mid Rates of RMB Against USD, 1979—2009

人民币/100美元
RMB per 100 USD

四、利用外资①

Ⅳ. Foreign Investment Utilization

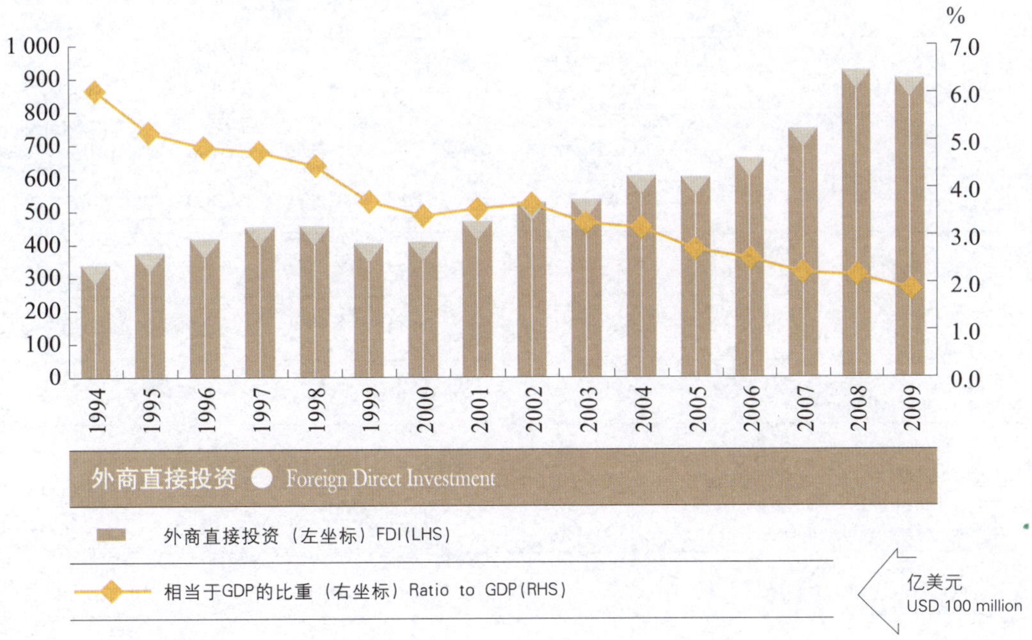

①资料来源：商务部。
Sources：Ministry of Commerce.

2009年利用外资

Foreign Direct Investment in 2009

单位：亿美元
Unit: USD 100 million

利用外资方式 Mode of Foreign Investment Utilization	本年批准外资项目数 Approved Foreign Investment Programs		本年实际使用外资 Actual Utilization of Foreign Investment	
	本年累计 Accumulative This Year	同比增长（%） Increase	本年累计 Accumulative This Year	同比增长（%） Increase
总计 Total	**23 435**	**-14.83**	**918.04**	**-3.62**
一、外商直接投资 Direct Foreign Investment	23 435	-14.83	900.33	-2.56
中外合资企业 Sino-Foreign Equity Joint Venture	4 283	-7.13	172.73	-0.26
中外合作企业 Sino-Foreign Contractual Joint Venture	390	-16.67	20.34	6.85
外资企业 Foreign Investment Enterprise	18 741	-16.32	686.82	-5.02
外商投资股份制 Stock-Holding by Foreign Investment	21	-44.74	20.44	137.86
合作开发 Cooperation Exploitation	0		0	
其他 Others	0		0	
二、外商其他投资 Other Foreign Investment	0		17.71	-38.02
对外发行股票 Issue Stocks to the Outside	0		1.62	110.27
国际租赁 International Tenancy	0		2.30	59.72
补偿贸易 Compensation Trade	0		0.13	-75.01
加工装配 Processing & Assembling	0		13.66	-47.14

注：统计数据为非金融领域。
Note: The data is subject to non-financial sectors.

五、外债①

V. External Debt

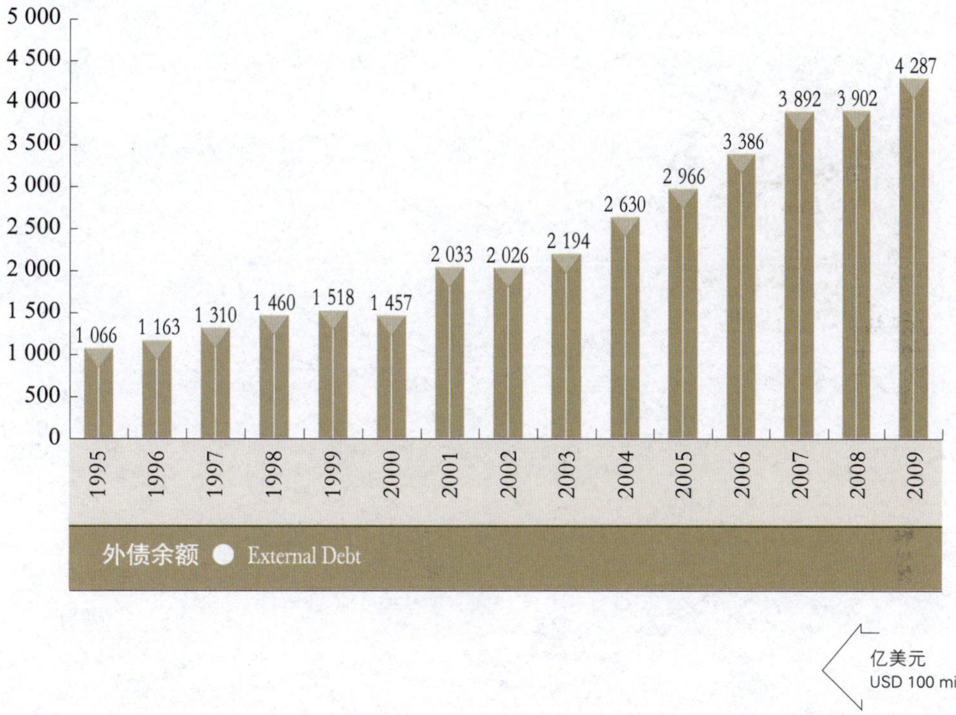

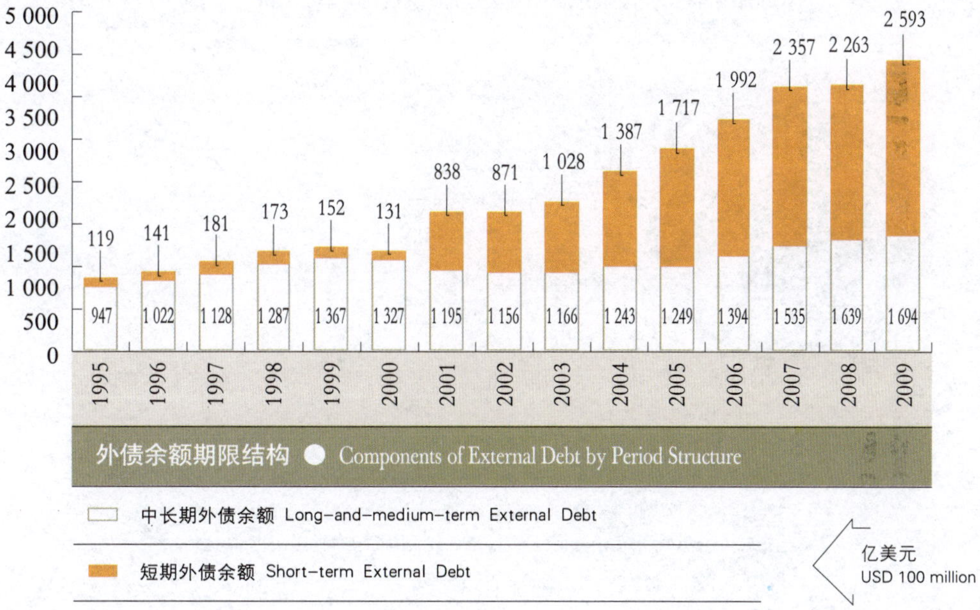

①资料来源：国家外汇管理局。
Sources: State Administration of Foreign Exchange.

2009年末外债余额期限结构
Components of External Debt by Period Structure, End of 2009

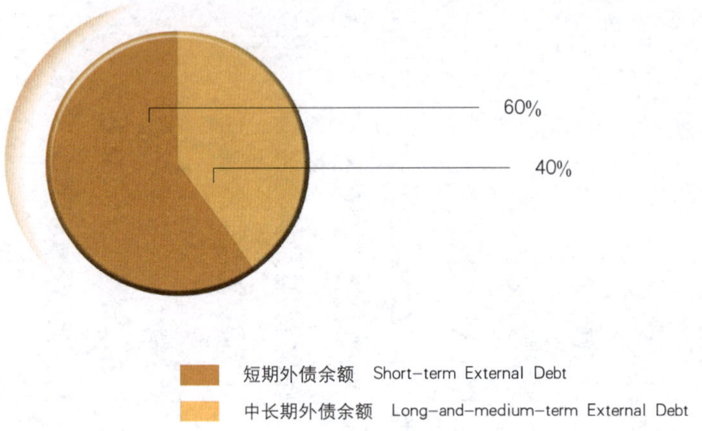

2009年末登记外债余额主体结构
Components of Registered External Debt by Type of Debtor, End of 2009

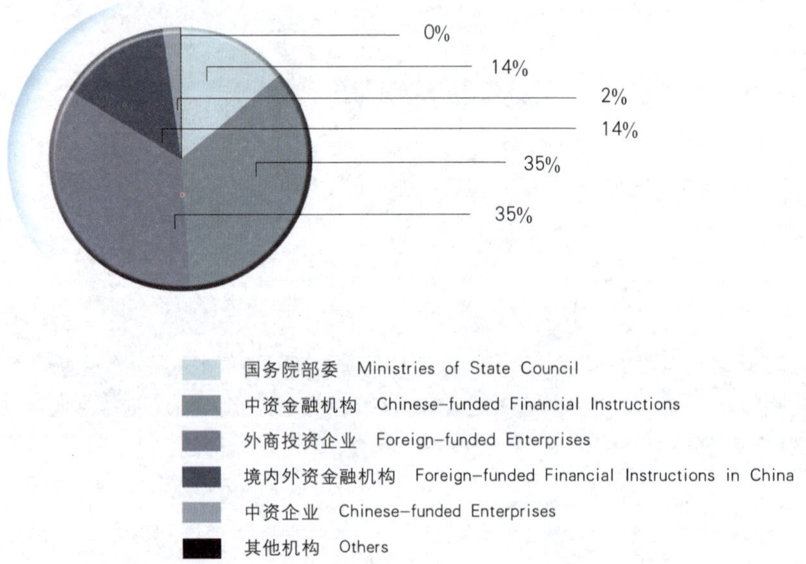

六、国际旅游①

Ⅵ. International Tourism

入境过夜旅游者人数和旅游外汇收入

Number of Inbound Stay-over Tourists and Foreign Exchange Income from Tourism

年份 Year	入境过夜旅游(万人次) Inbound Stay-over Tourists(10 000 persons)	旅游外汇收入（亿美元） Foreign Exchange Income from Tourism(USD 100 million)	年份 Year	入境过夜旅游（万人次） Inbound Stay-over Tourists(10 000 persons)	旅游外汇收入（亿美元） Foreign Exchange Income from Tourism(USD 100 million)
1978	71.6	2.63	1994	2 107.0	73.23
1979	152.9	4.49	1995	2 003.4	87.33
1980	350.0	6.17	1996	2 276.5	102.00
1981	367.7	7.85	1997	2 377.0	120.74
1982	392.4	8.43	1998	2 507.3	126.02
1983	379.1	9.41	1999	2 704.7	140.99
1984	514.1	11.31	2000	3 122.9	162.24
1985	713.3	12.50	2001	3 316.7	177.92
1986	900.1	15.31	2002	3 680.3	203.85
1987	1 076.0	18.62	2003	3 297.1	174.06
1988	1 236.1	22.47	2004	4 176.1	257.39
1989	936.1	18.60	2005	4 680.9	292.96
1990	1 048.4	22.18	2006	4 991.0	339.49
1991	1 246.4	28.45	2007	5 472.0	419.19
1992	1 651.2	39.47	2008	5 304.9	408.43
1993	1 898.2	46.83	2009	5 087.5	396.75

①资料来源：国家旅游局。
Sources：China National Tourism Administration.

七、世界经济增长状况①

Ⅶ. Growth of World Economy

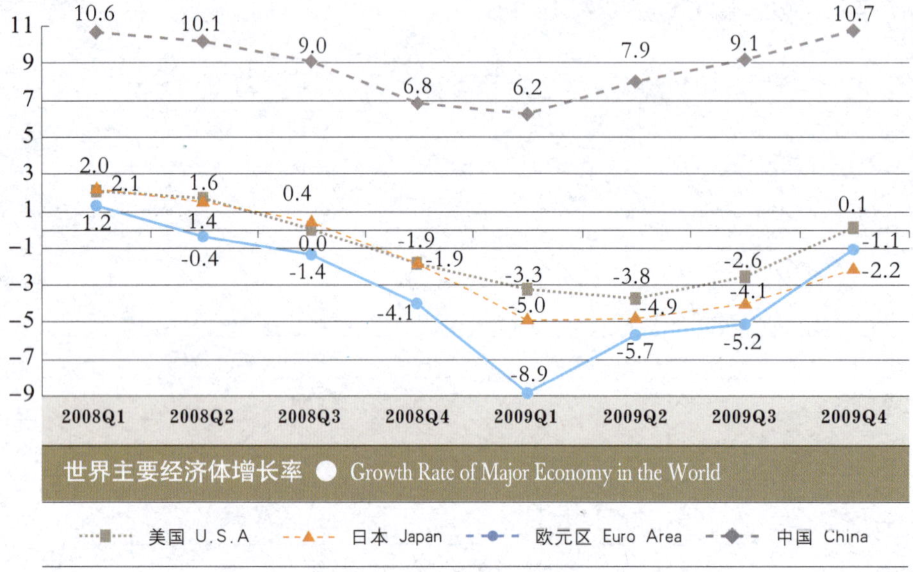

世界主要经济体增长率 ● Growth Rate of Major Economy in the World

经济增长率(%)
Growth Rate of Economy (%)

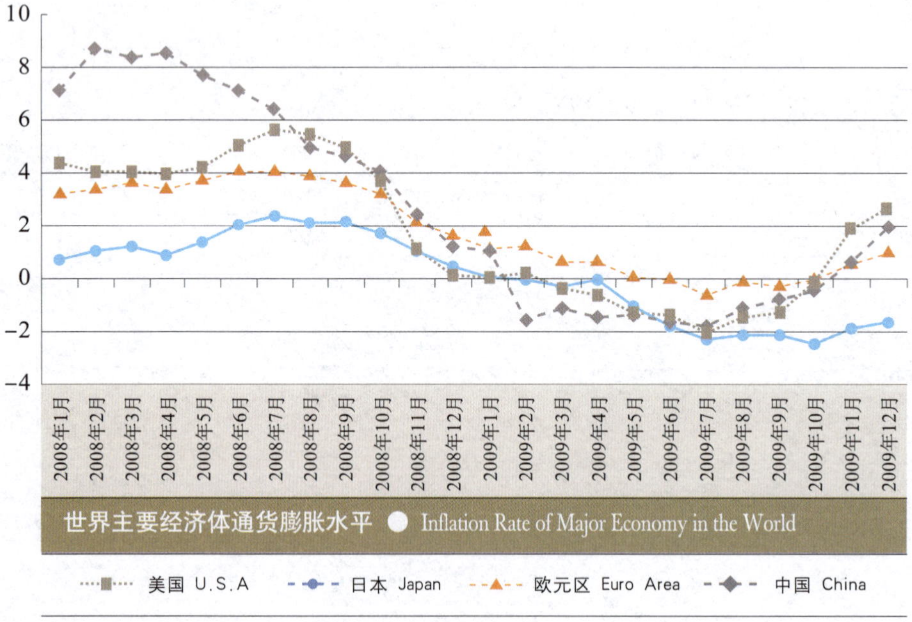

世界主要经济体通货膨胀水平 ● Inflation Rate of Major Economy in the World

居民消费价格指数
CPI

①资料来源：彭博资讯；CEIC Asia Database。
Sources: Bloomberg, CEIC Asia Database.

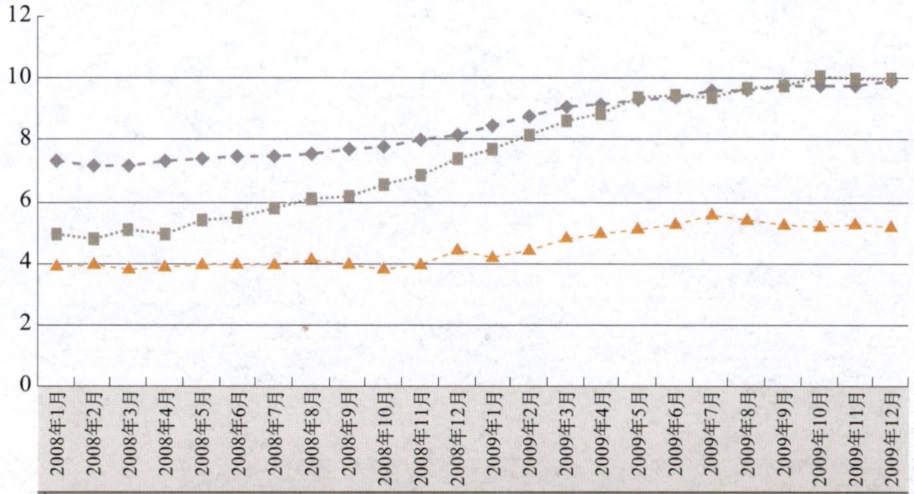

世界主要经济体就业状况 Employment of Major Economy in the World

美国 U.S.A 日本 Japan 欧元区 Euro Area

失业率(%)
Unemployment Rate (%)

八、国际金融市场状况①

Ⅷ. International Financial Market

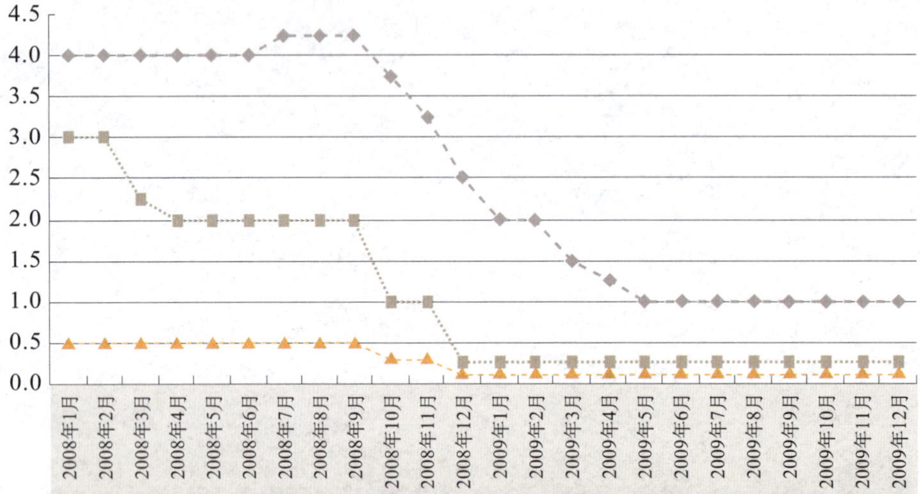

世界主要经济体基准利率 ● Basic Interest Rate of Major Economy in the World

美国 U.S.A　日本 Japan　欧元区 Euro Area

基准利率(%)
Basic Interest Rate (%)

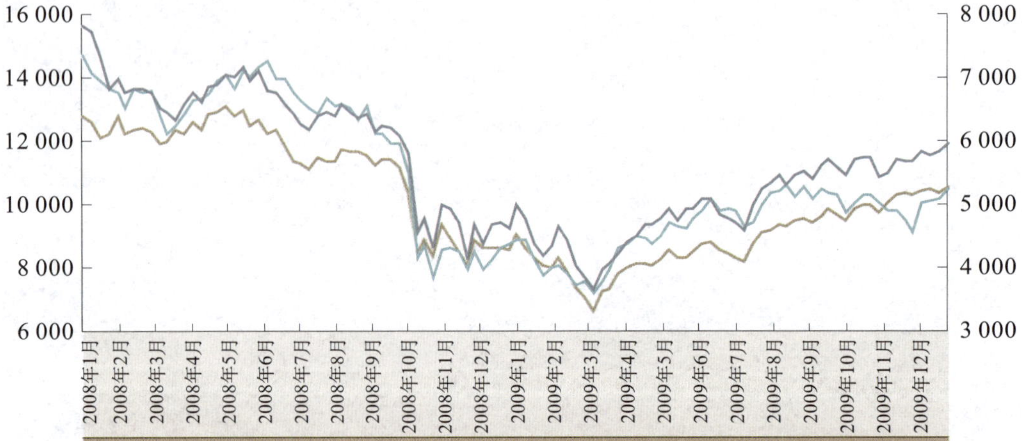

美国、德国及日本股票指数走势 ●
The Trend of Stock Indices in the Markets of U.S.A., Germany and Japan

道琼斯30种工业股票指数（左坐标）Dow Jones Industrial 30 Average(LHS)

日经225指数（左坐标）Nikkei 225(LHS)

法兰克福DAX指数（右坐标）Frankfurt DAX(RHS)

①资料来源：彭博资讯。
Sources：Bloomberg.

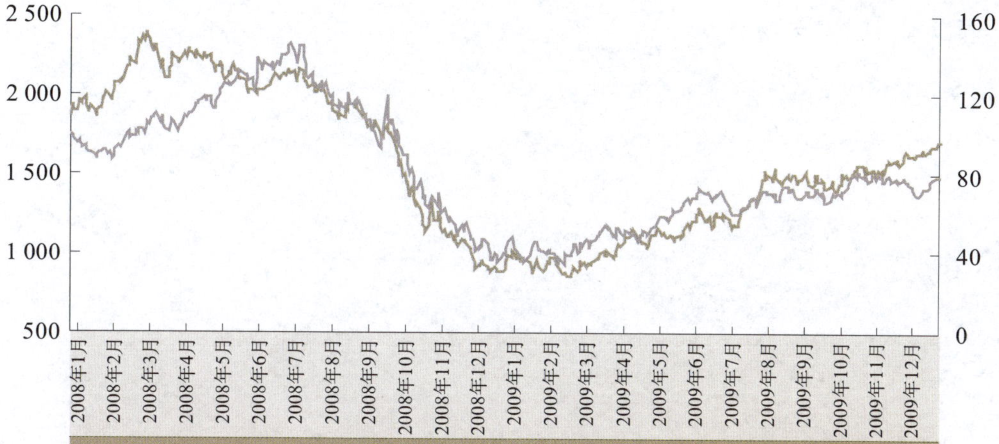

国际商品价格 ● Price of International Commodities

—— 高盛工业金属价格指数(总回报率)(左坐标) Goldman Sachs Industrial Metal Index Total Return (LHS)

—— 纽约商品交易所原油期货价格(右坐标) NYMEX Crude Oil Future Price(RHS)

美元/桶
USD/Barrel

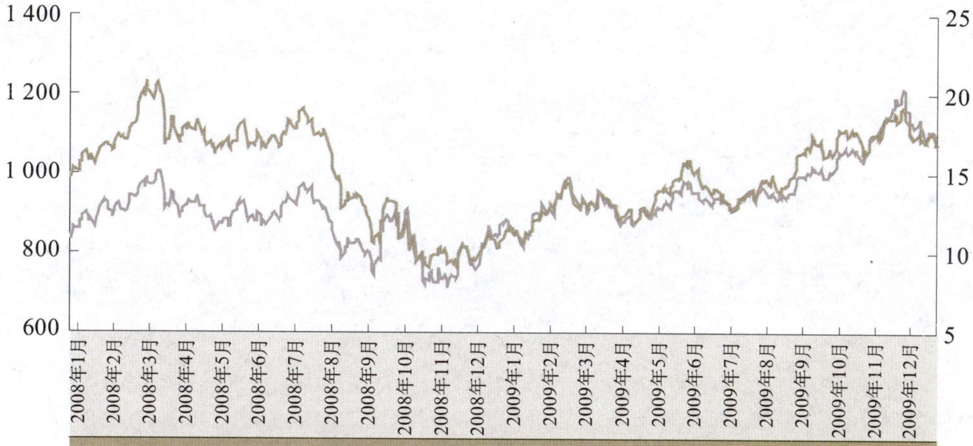

伦敦金属交易所金银价格 ● LME Gold and Silver Price

—— 黄金(左坐标) Gold(LHS)

—— 白银(右坐标) Silver(RHS)

美元/盎司
USD/Ounce